A Praxis of Nothingness in Education

T0299817

This book puts forward a "theory of Nothing" and shows how a praxis of "Nothing" can offer new possibilities for educational research and practice. Taking inspiration from Heidegger's and Wittgenstein's philosophy and with regards to phenomenology and language, the book indicates how nothing can be a condition for an educational technology.

The book translates the complex philosophical thinking of Heidegger and Wittgenstein into the realm of education studies, drawing on their perspectives to contribute to an understanding of how nothingness comes into being and how this relates to education. Arguing that nothingness addresses new possibilities for understanding and how we perceive the world and our place in it, the book theorises different aspects that can be included in a theory of Nothing, including indeterminateness, embodiment and how the inexpressible can be made expressible. The book presents vignettes and examples of educational practice and explores how nothing can show up in educational research, theory and practice.

Outlining a unique conceptualisation of nothingness in education, the book will be of great interest to academics, researchers and post-graduate students in the field of educational philosophy and educational theory.

Håvard Åsvoll is Professor at Nord University, Norway.

Routledge International Studies in the Philosophy of Education

A Praxis of Nothingness in Education

On Heidegger and Wittgenstein

Håvard Åsvoll

Routledge
Taylor & Francis Group

LONDON AND NEW YORK

First published 2022
by Routledge
2 Park Square, Milton Park, Abingdon, Oxon OX14 4RN

and by Routledge
605 Third Avenue, New York, NY 10158

*Routledge is an imprint of the Taylor & Francis Group, an
informa business*

© 2022 Håvard Åsvoll

British Library Cataloguing-in-Publication Data
A catalogue record for this book is available from the British
Library

Library of Congress Cataloging-in-Publication Data
A catalog record has been requested for this book

ISBN: 978-1-032-11938-0 (hbk)
ISBN: 978-1-032-11939-7 (pbk)
ISBN: 978-1-003-22223-1 (ebk)

DOI: 10.4324/9781003222231

Typeset in Times New Roman
by Apex CoVantage, LLC

Contents

Part 1
Introduction and theorising nothing

1　Introduction

As a beginning, both L. Wittgenstein and M. Heidegger say something essential with regard to this book:

> *I am not interested in constructing a building, so much as in having a perspicuous view of the foundations of possible buildings.*
>
> (Wittgenstein, 1980, p. 7)

> *Everywhere everything is ordered to stand by, to be immediately at hand, indeed to stand there just so that it may be on call for a further ordering. Whatever is ordered about in this way has its own standing. We call it the standing-reserve [Bestand]. . . . Thus . . . Where Enframing holds sway, the regulating and securing of standing in reserve marks all. They no longer even allow their own fundamental characteristic of revealing to appear.*
>
> (Heidegger, 1977, p. 17 and 26)

This book is about the relationship between technology and the theory of nothing in educational practice. The philosophy of Martin Heidegger and Ludwig Wittgenstein is used to examine and articulate this relationship. The aforementioned quotes indicate that educational participants (including researchers) should use technology (the standing reserve) not only as an instrument at hand but also as a "way of revealing". And Wittgenstein's thinking through architecture gives abstract thought a concrete quality that renders possibilities more visible or, in Heideggerian terms, shows the potential of nothing as the groundless ground of possibilities.[1]

In other words, technology and the theory of nothing can be something that we are embedded in and use as a kind of *praxis of the possible* through everyday experiences, in educational practice and in educational contexts. Here, technology should be understood in a broad sense and as a dominant framework for educational practice. This means that the term encompasses

DOI: 10.4324/9781003222231-2

control tools, structural frameworks, popular organisational methods, teaching, (theories of) learning and a delivery logic that ultimately rests on a kind of (theoretical) understanding of knowledge. Technology consists of tools and artefacts that are efficient and ready for use and that can be mobilised and used with the least possible friction by school principals, teachers, pupils, politicians, researchers and institutions. Key terms in this context are learning outcomes, quality assurance, implementation, production (i.e. credits, publication points), control, evaluation, behavioural change, competence (goals), educational quality, etc. This technology is a complex and multifaceted phenomenon that is manifested at several different levels of educational practice, including (1) individual propositions (i.e. new self-understanding and new possible worlds), (2) reflective constructs (some theory, for instance relating to learning, didactics/teaching), (3) regional understandings/ontologies of different kinds of beings (art, law, economics, sociology, psychology), (4) the overall understanding of being that gives unity to an epoch, in modernity termed technology (*das Gestell*) and, finally, (5) the formal conditions (phenomenological) for the understanding of being whatsoever.

Building on the claim that, left unchallenged, technology represents an attempt to shut down Nothing and freedom in educational practice (including educational research), Heidegger and Wittgenstein together offer an alternative route through their philosophy of lost-your-way or Nothing (Not-being-at-home). In lost-your-way as a theory of nothing, there is always room for questions such as "Where am I going? Where is my home? How can you become what you are?"[2] since being is approached ontologically, emphasising (new) ways of being rather than final truth (*veritas*) and fixed ways of doing things. According to the theory of nothing and in line with the intention behind this book, every educational participant has the capacity to resist, confront and make personal meaning out of technology. As such, emphasis is placed on "here and now" situations, being(-there) and the indeterminate understanding that is in play in educational practice, rather than on seeking consensus and a laundry list of competences and best practice as a necessary outcome.

The importance of performance and praxis is key here, in a technology (theory)-nothing (praxis) perspective. For instance, researchers learn to conduct advanced research by engaging in research, not by reading about it or attending courses about how research can be conducted. More is required to become a good concert pianist than just notes; being and performing in a stage setting require the pianist to master skills that have become second nature. A teacher does not become a good teacher just by knowing everything about didactic theory; the practice of teaching is also about being alert in unpredictable learning situations where he or she can draw on previous experiences. A professional football coach must know more than just how to analyse play and have a theoretical knowledge of football; giving feedback in coaching situations that suddenly arise is about the capability of being intuitively attentive to certain aspects of the training. These four situations can be said to be characterised by a certain professional practice, where theoretical/technological knowledge is only necessary to the extent that it is part of the performance and praxis.[3]

One particularly important factor in this context is not just how acquired experience and technology/knowledge are performed and *applied* in situations that require action, but also how the practitioner (the teacher, principal, pupil, student, researcher) creates a new understanding and knowledge that rests on nothing. It is about creating or not creating experiences and a new self-understanding when faced with routine praxis, situations requiring action and unexpected events. New (nothing) experiences that either do not necessarily "fit" already established theoretical/technological knowledge bases, or that are (temporarily) inaccessible for theorisation/articulation, can nonetheless be decisive in an educational practice.

For example, even in such a theoretical exercise as writing this book, (self-)insights can pop up that have not been thoroughly thought through and technologically prepared for use but that change meaning in this writing context. It would not be possible to write if I constantly had to reflect on all the rules and technology that are necessary to master the art of writing. Understanding arises at the same time as or just after the performance/recognition of the previous insight. In other words, praxis/performance is not something you can just learn about, but it is also something you can learn and experience through (nothing).

These are (nothing) experiences that often precede our theoretical knowledge and lie behind a technological world that is always ready for use. The theory of nothing is about pre-epistemological and often pre-language elements that challenge our (self-)understanding and way of being. As a point of departure, it is possible to outline six aspects that can be included in a theory of Nothing.[4]

- Indeterminateness – the term horizon[5] may describe the indeterminate nature and always already potential of nothing, which includes some form of passive compulsion; hence, expressions like "We do not decide our experiences ourselves!? Experiences force themselves on us!" This enforced indeterminateness is further illustrated in a radical way in the statement: "*Höher als die Wirklichkeit steht die Möglichkeit*" (Heidegger, 1962, p. 38). It is discussed in projection and letting-go in Chapter 6.
- Personal[6] – this aspect makes it possible to see the connection between nothingness and personal experience. Experience (*erfahrung*)[7] as an

unpredictable journey and a hazardous life project may inherit the openness of nothing. The most important thing is that Heidegger (1968) did
not seek an understanding or mere knowledge, but a special kind of inner
experience of anxiety, which is the feeling of existence as the coming-to-
be of newness. It is discussed in Chapter 6.

- Embodiment[8] – embodied sense of sight.
- Skills-based – skills as the utilisation of tools (hence, the centrality of
  tools and equipmentality) in Heidegger (*Dasein*'s everyday relationship
  to objects) and Wittgenstein (the familiarity of seeing something as
  something). It is discussed in Chapter 6.
- Intimacy-based – this aspect could shed light on the relationship
  between dwelling or form of life and not-being-at-home (nothing). It is
  elaborated in Chapter 6 and discussed in Chapter 7.
- Can break free of the language – here, the crucial point is how the
  "inexpressible" can be expressible and vice versa. As an apparent
  double-bind paradox, this is further investigated in Chapter 6, focusing
  on the difference between showing (Zeigen) itself in the world rather
  than being sayable. Hence, saying and showing are two modes of nothing. It is discussed in *Being-reserved* and *Being-blank* in Chapter 7.

It is a fundamental premise for this book that it assumes that praxis is an
important factor. Theoretical knowledge that is abstract, possible to for-
mulate and systematic rests on the practitioner's praxis (cf. being-in-the-
world and form of lives). This means that the meaning and possibilities
for understanding that lie in an articulated and systematic theory must be
reflected or thrown back into a concrete, action-requiring (skills-based)
and unpredictable (intimate) praxis. In other words, it should always be
possible at some point to see the abstract (theory) in the context of and
interweave it with the concrete (praxis), even though it is far from always
given how this should and can be done. My main intention with this book
is, therefore, to clarify – to unravel knots and significant links between
theory/technology and praxis/nothing. With the help of different theoreti-
cal/philosophical and empirical focuses, different aspects and interwoven
elements are presented from a theory/technology – praxis (nothing) perspective. In brief, the book is an attempt to highlight the mutual dependence that exists between technology and nothing – an interdependence
that is not necessarily characterised by a harmonious balance and a
controlling reason, but where the parties contribute to each other's development and are contentious and unpredictable. In a way, the distinction
between theory (technology) and praxis (nothing) is misleading precisely
because nothing (Being-there) can be present in both theory and praxis.
Theory and praxis can thereby represent two different modes of nothing.

The result is that theory/technology is also regarded as a form of praxis, that is praxis is a fundamental process that realises theory and praxis (i.e. skills). The main point, as Heidegger (1962) points out, is that praxis should never be conceived as being directed by or in the service of theory (theoria). Praxis is our concern (*Besorgen*) with the entities we encounter, and beyond that, it is concern for the Being (and hence Nothing).

Reading Heidegger together with Wittgenstein is encouraged by some intriguing similarities between Heidegger's and Wittgenstein's perspectives on seeing the world and the relations human beings enter into with it. It is argued that both Heidegger and Wittgenstein hoped for an existence that would be not only sensitive to the significance of everydayness (both to the things created by man and to those brought forth by nature) but also open to receiving the world as an extraordinary gift that exceeds human comprehension (more on this in Chapter 5). Hence, comparing Wittgenstein's and Heidegger's respective views illuminates them both.

In other words, this is also an attempt to unravel knots in our (linguistic) interaction with the technology (theory)-nothing (praxis) dynamics without succumbing to the tyranny of either theory or praxis. There are many ways of approaching these problems, and Gilbert Ryle (1949), for example, sheds light on a conceptual pitfall in his classic book *The Concept of Mind*. This means that using an educational technology that rests on a technological and entitative language makes it easy to make a "category mistake" (Ryle, 1949), since concepts can obscure that "not merely [has] some performance . . . been gone through, but also that something has been brought off by the agent going through it" (p. 125).

For example, terms such as learning outcome and (planned) teaching may be confused with learning itself. In other words, used entitatively, concepts merely denote the *outcomes* of an indeterminate and tentative process, unfolding *within*, that is being-in-the-world (Heidegger, 1962) or forms of life (Wittgenstein, 2005). However, for teachers, students and researchers to achieve these outcomes, they must somehow make an effort to achieve them that is not fully captured by the language of technology:

> *A person's performance is described as careful or skillful, if in his operations he is ready to detect and correct lapses, to repeat and improve upon successes, to profit from the examples of others and so forth. He applies criteria in performing critically, that is, in trying to get things right.*

> (Ryle, 1949, p. 29)

In other words, such efforts or "tryings" may result in appropriate achievements if different strands of influence – many involving practitioners' openness to the developing nature of details in their surroundings – are intertwined in an appropriate manner.

There are several ways to avoid making category mistakes. For example, to better capture more of the complexity of the process at hand (Tsoukas & Hatch, 2001), "categorically based knowing" should be balanced with "perceptually based knowing" (Weick, 2007, p. 18). Such a balance is achieved when scholars adopt the "e-prime mind-set" (Weick, 2001, p. 18) in their theorising, which helps them to include more context, situational specificity and agency. However, a theory of nothing may also illuminate another possibility, the uncanny feeling of not-being-at-home anymore and hence the potential of a renewed (ontological) understanding.

In order to address such issues, this book is divided into different chapters with several sections. Firstly, an introduction to the Nothing perspective is presented (1), eventually followed by a description of what technology as the companion of nothing may look like in education (3). In Chapter 2, four arguments are presented for the relevance of Nothing. Thereafter, Wittgenstein and Heidegger's relationship to education is explored (4). Finally, I examine how parts of Heidegger and Wittgenstein's philosophy can be combined in the quest for a theory of nothing (5). The second part provides a description of how to move towards a theory of "Nothing" in educational practice. This includes an introduction to selected parts of Heidegger and Wittgenstein's philosophy. Thereafter, vignettes and examples of educational practice are presented based on pivotal aspects of nothing (e.g. technology and projection) (Chapter 7). Chapter 8 explains the implications of a theory of Nothing for prevailing educational research, theory and education. However, I first describe and examine some of the threads connecting theory and practice. It is important to focus more on the theory-practice dimension(s), because their different perspectives shed light on major controversies in the educational and pedagogical domain.

Theory and praxis in pedagogy

The relationship between technology (theory) and nothing (praxis) and the problems associated with it can be examined from an educational perspective in several ways. By asking different types of questions, light can be shed on various aspects of the theory-praxis relationship: What is it best to learn in the educational system and what is it best to learn in the workplace? To what extent is there an interplay or a conflict between theory and praxis in different arenas, for example between (scholastic) education and non-scholastic settings? In current pedagogical research, there is a debate that, to put it simply, can be said to give two distinct answers to these questions. The first answer comes from the scholastic tradition. The predominant scholastic or school tradition favours knowledge about facts and rules that can be exhaustively expressed in language and communicated in writing (Kvale & Nielsen, 2004). The main idea is that knowledge is found in textbooks, teaching, lectures, and scientific and theoretical competence that can later be transferred to and applied in practice in the workplace.

The fundamental "applicable" and scholastic assumption lies in the philosophy of education considered solely as an applied field. At first glance, this may seem an attractive way of thinking, especially at a time when philosophy and the humanities, in general, are under pressure to prove their practical importance (cf. Chapter 3). Keeping the interwoven theory-practice (praxis) perspective in mind, there is every reason to be cautious here as regards the idea of philosophy as something that is "applied" (especially with regard to nothing phenomenology). This can be understood in relation to the pairing of "theory" and "practice", with the implication that there is a clear separation between the two. This generates an instrumental conception, like a picture that holds us captive with respect to what the work of philosophy should be, that is, philosophy represents the theory (conceived as conceptual analysis and theory building), which is then applied in practice. An extreme version of this view in relation to education was provided by J. Wilson, who argued that the only thing that philosophy could do with respect to education was to clarify such basic concepts as teaching, learning, authority and education itself (Standish, 2006). These concepts would then form the basis for the development of educational policy and practice (more on this issue in Chapter 3, where I argue that Wilson's main assumption is still very much alive in today's educational technology). In other words, here is the philosopher/researcher doing the serious theoretical work, and there is the practitioner (i.e. the teacher) whose job will be to apply these ideas.

This is just a snapshot that represents a scholastic tradition. The message is: a theory-based education and theory-based entry to practising a profession enjoys a privileged status. The other answer is a critique of the scholastic perspective. From a non-scholastic perspective, consisting of theories about praxis communities and apprenticeship systems (Lave & Wenger, 1991), the reflective practitioner (Schön, 2002), "embodied philosophical" learning (Jespersen, 2004), the intuitive expert (Dreyfus & Dreyfus, 2004) and others, schools or the scholastic practicing of theory-based teaching and learning is criticised. This perspective could be an attempt to follow up Ryle (1971, p. 225): *"The uneducated public erroneously equates education with the imparting of knowing-that. Philosophers have not hitherto made it very clear what its error is."* From a non-scholastic perspective, it is important to pursue a theoretical alternative to "knowing-that", or context-independent/ theoretical rules and insights. The fact that philosophers have not succeeded in correcting such an erroneous conclusion on the part of the uneducated public, as Ryle (1971) claims, is also subject to debate today, a debate that pedagogical research still struggles with. For example, as it pertains to the teaching profession, teachers' knowledge is often thought to be largely tacit (Guerriero, 2017) and hence not subject to theoretical or know-that knowledge. Theories such as activity theory or expansive learning (Engeström & Sannino, 2010) oppose a rigid knowing-that entry, because they closely link the creation of knowledge with learning (focusing, in particular, on professional communities) and reinforce the argument that new knowledge is produced through the professional activities of teachers. Engeström and Sannino (2010) use the metaphor of "expansive learning" to highlight that professional learning is often not about learning something that is already known but about designing new activities that merge with the acquisition of knowledge.

To simplify somewhat, we can say that these are two theoretical perspectives on praxis that stand in opposition to each other and that each criticises the other's limitations and weaknesses. From a scholastic perspective, a person can have learned many rules, theories and principles without knowing how they should be applied in specific practical situations. From a non-scholastic perspective, a person can engage in advanced actions without being capable of formulating, reflecting on or theorising about them. It is possible to take sides with one of the two main perspectives, and it is possible to argue (normatively/politically and descriptively) that the one side's limitations and weaknesses are preferable to those of the other.

As mentioned, the intention is to avoid a mutually exclusive antagonism. Theoretical distance, reflection and analysis, and praxis grounded in understanding and intuition can instead be examined as fruitful, exciting and mutually dependent aspects of a pedagogical and educational praxis. This means that there is hope that knowledge will neither remain forever within the realm of nothing, that is left exclusively to non-reflective praxis, nor that understanding and knowledge will be left to know-all theories and reflections that result in a paralysing praxis. That said, the book primarily focuses on how theory and praxis can interact and how technology and nothing "processes" can work together. The value of this mutual dependence is the primary point of departure for identifying possibilities for a theory of nothing (hence, being-there/Nothing may occur both theoretically and in practice).

It is crucial to note that both Heidegger and Wittgenstein oppose practical comportment, which includes problem-solving, in terms that are grounded in the Cartesian subject-object split, which adopts the view that the world can be known, controlled and mastered. And this has crucial implications for the way in which contemporary education views the unfolding of the continuum of, and relationship between, theory and practice. However, Heidegger (1962) assures us that "practical behaviour" is not "atheoretical" in the sense of "sightless". It is an oversimplification of things to simply say that in theoretical behaviour we observe, while in practical affairs we act, and that action must employ theoretical cognition if it not to remain blind. So far, this has been an attempt to frame some of the complexity of the theory of nothing. In the following, I will explain some of the possible (counter)arguments for the relevance of the theory of nothing.

Its relevance to our perspective on the theory of nothing can be summarised in four arguments: a societal argument, a research argument, a moral argument and a knowledge argument.

Notes

1   Whether Wittgenstein adequately deals with Heidegger in an implicit philosophical sense and vice versa (that is to say, if they may illuminate each other), or not, depends on whether we favour a "resolute" or "continuation" reading of both (this is a question about how much continuity there is between their earliest thoughts and the later philosophy. I argue the latter "continuation" reading, because to divide Wittgenstein and Heidegger into sharp drawn periods is unhelpful, as it hides from our view the (genealogical) traces of their articulations and revisions and hence their possible relation with each other.

2   This peculiar question from Heidegger (1962) makes sense because Being-there (Da-sein) *is* what it becomes. In other words, in one sense, Dasein always exists in such a manner that it is "not yet".

3   For Heidegger (2000), this experience of "performance" is *the empowering experiencing of living experience that takes itself along* (p. 99). Heidegger (1968) equates gaining an awareness of this existential singularity with learning to swim in a river; *"We shall never learn what 'is called' swimming . . . or what it 'calls for,' by reading a treatise on swimming. Only the leap into the river tells us what is called swimming"* (p. 21). If one doesn't make this leap, then *"one is supposed to learn swimming, but only goes meandering on the riverbank, converses about the murmuring of the stream, and talks about the cities and towns the river passes. This guarantees that the spark never flashes"* (Heidegger, 1984, p. 7).

4   Why is Nothing sometimes written with a capital N? It may seem like a logical violation to switch from the negative existential form to the noun. Heidegger himself makes this alteration by simultaneously marking the noun with a capital first letter (*Nichts*) and uses this difference in order to show that *Nichts* is not a quantification over entities, that is a quantification that runs *over a range of beings*. The reason for this is that Being-Nothing is not related to beings according to a logical (quantifiable) relationship but is related to them through an ontological relationship. Hence, to foresee being is one thing, while Being is quite another (why beings are).

5   Horizon as a metaphor expresses the breadth of vision that a person who is trying to understand must have, and where there can be no standing outside the given horizon (cf. Wittgenstein's language games, which transcribe into horizons when the comparison is focused on the aspect of constraint. This may have limitations:

"The world is *my* world: this is manifest in the fact that the limits of language mean the limits of *my* world") (Wittgenstein, 2005, paragraph 5.62). In short, for Heidegger (1962), horizon denotes phenomena that stand out from an underlying unity, in the sense of what limits and encloses, and in so doing discloses or makes available understanding.

6 Heidegger (1962) does not refer to the psychological subject or personality as the centre of being-in-the-world. Firstly, in ontological terms, comes Dasein's openness, and, secondly, the "self-subsistence" of Existenz which, in turn, rests on nothingness (decentering).

7 Heidegger's (1962, 1968) Erfahrung is the feeling of being created ex nihilo. The "er-" of "Erfahrung" is an etymological variant of the "ur-" of "ursprünglich". In *Contributions to Philosophy*, Heidegger (1968) uses the device of hyphenation to emphasise the connotation of pure origination, writing "er-fahren", "er-fährt" and "Er-fahrung" (cf. pp. 160, 391 and 483). "Fahren" means "to drive" or "to move", so "Er-fahren" explicitly connotes the feeling of being moved by the power of origination. Heidegger (1968) makes it clear that his Er-fahrung is the feeling of the Ur-sprung of new existence.

8 Heidegger's talk of "dwelling", "paths", "place", "Dasein", and so on clearly refers to embodiment. However, he avoids the terminology of the body. There are several reasons for this; for more details, see Overgaard (2004) on how Heidegger is indeed struggling to bring out Dasein's corporeal situatedness in the world. Embodiment is also central to Wittgenstein in overcoming Cartesianism. For example, he stresses in Philosophical Investigations that "*It is a human being of flesh and blood that perceives, thinks, feels pain and fear, goes shopping, plays tennis and does mental arithmetic – it is neither an 'immaterial soul' nor a 'material body'*" (Wittgenstein, 2001, paragraphs 573 and 286).

References

Dreyfus, H., & Dreyfus, S. (2004). Mesterlære og eksperters læring. In K. Nielsen & S. Kvale (Eds.), *Mesterlære: Læring som sosial praksis* (pp. 52–69). Oslo: Gyldendal.

Engeström, Y., & Sannino, A. (2010). Studies of Expansive Learning: Foundations, Findings and Future Challenges. *Educational Research Review*, 5, pp. 1–24.

Guerriero, S. (Ed.). (2017). *Pedagogical Knowledge and the Changing Nature of the Teaching Profession*. Paris: OECD Publishing. http://doi.org/10.1787/9789264270695-en

Heidegger, H. (1977). The Question Concerning Technology. In W. Lovitt (Ed.), *The Question Concerning Technology and Other Essays*. New York: Harper & Row Publishers.

Heidegger, M. (1962). *Being and Time*. New York: Harper & Row.

Heidegger, M. (1968). *What is Called Thinking?* (J. G. Gray, Trans.). New York: Harper and Row.

Heidegger, M. (1984). *The Metaphysical Foundations of Logic* (M. Heim, Trans.). Bloomington: Indiana University Press.

Heidegger, M. (2000). *Towards the Definition of Philosophy* (T. Sandler, Trans.). London: The Athlone Press.

Jespersen, E. (2004). Idrettens kroppslige mesterlære. In K. Nielsen & S. Kvale (Eds.), *Mesterlære: Læring som sosial praksis* (pp. 137–148). Oslo: Ad Notam Gyldendal.

Kvale, S., & Nielsen, K. (2004). Mesterlære som aktuell læringsform. In K. Nielsen & S. Kvale (eds.), *Mesterlære: Læring som sosial praksis* (pp. 17–33). Oslo: Ad Notam Gyldendal.

Lave, J., & Wenger, E. (1991). *Situated Learning: Legitimate Peripheral Participation*. Cambridge and New York: Cambridge University Press.

Overgaard, S. (2004). Heidegger on Embodiment. *Journal of the British Society for Phenomenology*, 35(2), pp. 116–131.

Ryle, G. (1949). *The Concept of Mind*. London: Methuen.

Ryle, G. (1971). *Collected Papers* (Vol. 1). London: Hutchinson & Co.

Schön, D. (2002). *The Reflective Practitioner: How Professionals Think in Action*. New York: Basic Books.

Standish, P. (2006). John Wilson's Confused 'Perspectives on the Philosophy of Education'. *Oxford Review of Education*, 32(2), pp. 269–279.

Tsoukas, H., & Hatch, M. J. (2001). Complex Thinking, Complex Practice: The Case for a Narrative Approach to Organizational Complexity. *Human Relations*, 54, pp. 979–1013.

Weick, K. E. (2001). *Making Sense of the Organization*. Oxford: Blackwell Publishing Ltd.

Weick, K. E. (2007). The Generative Properties of Richness. *Academy of Management Journal*, 50(1), pp. 14–19.

Wittgenstein, L. (1980). *Culture and Value* (G. H. Von Wright & H. Nyman, Eds.; P. Winch, Trans.). Chicago, IL: The University of Chicago Press.

Wittgenstein, L. (2001). *Philosophical Investigations*. Oxford: Blackwell Publishers.

2 Four arguments for a theory of nothing

The societal argument

As part of academic pedagogy, phenomenological research (for instance, on nothing education) and practice are also influenced by society's requirement that they must be useful. The following is said about pedagogy and the demands on teacher knowledge, based on the situation in the 21st century: *more is required to be able to improve pedagogy, teacher education and professional development of teachers*; hence, the expectations of what the new pedagogy can achieve in our globalised world are very high (Guerriero, 2017, p. 15). Pedagogy is still endeavouring to meet these expectations by promising better learning; it is expected to solve discipline problems, counteract the dissolution of norms and values in society, prevent motivation failure, etc. It is, therefore, unsurprising that a focus on Nothing in a pedagogical perspective must also address a societal benefit argument. From such a perspective, it is expected that the pedagogical "effects" of Nothing must be documented, clarified and perhaps also subject to quantifiable efficiency and evaluation requirements. It is a question of how an understanding of Nothing should/can lead to knowledge and learning, and how it should be justified and defended in everything from schools' praxis to activities in the workplace. However, the value of praxis and its hidden Nothing "resources" do not seem to enjoy support, neither in the prevailing research trends nor in a policy perspective. It is possible to see some interest in the educational sector as well as in the business community, where the value and potential of nothing can, at best, only be assessed in terms of its immediate knowledge benefit/learning outcome and from an economic perspective. This means that Nothing and its ensuing praxis learning and learning in work contexts only have (societal) value as a hidden resource if it is possible to refine and sell it as quickly as possible within given limits. In this context, the driving force could be to achieve a competitive advantage by raising awareness of nothingness as a phenomenon, which, in turn, could

DOI: 10.4324/9781003222231-3

improve the quality and productivity of practical work. It is possible here that the world is seen as unrefined in objective terms, where there are a lot of raw materials just waiting to be converted into "cash values". Regardless of whether you sympathise with the view that there is such a direct connection between nothing/learning/pedagogy and the interests of modern capitalism, the underlying reasoning is nonetheless interesting. It is not knowledge of principles, strategies and theories that results in various competitive advantages, but whether one is in a situation that can stimulate awareness of nothing (praxis), which, in turn, can contribute to economic profit. A phenomenological objection here would be that the value of nothing as a phenomenon is not primarily extrinsic and quantifiable (economically, in terms of learning), like a procedure for fixing things or a technique for knowledge development. A stronger objection is that this nothing phenomenology is only about how you think about yourself and your education in a totally new way. It is not about helping you to do things better, it is about helping you to think about your place among the things you are doing.

The research argument

In light of society's constantly reiterated demand (usually strongly economically motivated) that learning must be improved in general and that the quality (of learning) must be improved in both educational institutions and forms of teaching (Guerriero, 2017), it is possible to identify a need to conduct research on and examine (alternative) phenomenological nothing and learning aspects of situations that do not necessarily occur in formal scholastic/organised settings. A focus on this need is nothing new, Resnick (1987), for example, says:

> There is growing evidence, then, that not only may schooling not contribute in a direct and obvious way to performance outside school but also that knowledge acquired outside school is not always used to support in-school learning. Schooling is coming to look increasingly isolated from the rest of what we do.
>
> (p. 15)

Even though it is more than 30 years since Resnick (1987) pointed out the need for descriptive and analytical investigations of learning that can provide us with a suitable framework for understanding learning processes in their natural environment and shed light on the connections between scholastic and non-scholastic performance, learning and "learnification" still occupy a strong position in the understanding of education as an isolated sphere (see Chapter 3) (despite the development of new "situated" theoretical and empirical perspectives, i.e. Brown, Collins, & Duguid, 1989; Engeström, 1996; Lave & Wenger, 1991; Schön, 1987; Dreyfus & Dreyfus, 1986; Wertsch, 1991). Calling for research interest in nothing education in its natural environment turns the spotlight on the performers and the *performance* of (prior) understanding of vocational knowledge in the workplace and professional contexts where knowledge is also practised, applied and, not least, created and acquired. This is about increased recognition of the significance that personal knowledge and first-person experiences can have in terms of the performance of knowledge. This means a research focus that no longer underestimates the importance of concepts such as experience, praxis, intuition, skills and embodied knowledge. Traditionally, research has predominantly either ignored or taken a negative view of these terms from a knowledge perspective – as a kind of knowledge that is unreliable, far too subjective and irrational.

From a nothing perspective, more research is not needed if its ideal is a prescriptive, objective (independent of praxis) knowledge that can be applied in all concrete situations as long as it is systematic enough, sufficiently standardised and verifiable. Instead of waiting for more prescriptive research, textbook templates and possibly artificial intelligence, the focus is describing uncertain situations, praxis that requires action and, in part, hidden/tacit nothing aspects that are characterised precisely by being performed (cf. Chapter 7). This line of reasoning can also be reflected in a moral reason or a moral perspective as regards the focus on research participants.

The moral argument

Useful knowledge is no longer just what can be formulated explicitly and verbally, but what can be practised. Praxis is understood not just as the application of theoretical knowledge but also as an insight and "theory" in itself. Therefore, it is important to be aware of the approach to the reduction of practical comportment to "theories", as we find in the notion of the "expert/educator" problem-solver in Darling-Hammond and Bransford (2005), who possesses the skill to transform "knowing-how" into "knowing that". This sort of logic runs into trouble when "facts and rules 'discovered' in the detached attitude do not capture the skills manifest in circumspective coping" (Dreyfus & Dreyfus, 1986).

The moral argument, therefore, emphasises the importance of describing this praxis and its knowledge. The descriptions are based on the research participants' first-person experiences, self-understanding and performance. It is a fundamental principle here that the concepts on the basis of which the research participants must lead their lives cannot be ignored. A "theory" of nothing must describe what is experienced (the participant perspective) and, if relevant, explain why that is not how it is experienced. Taylor (1985), among others, points out that such descriptions must be tested in light of the quality they give rise to, that is that *"we must therefore be able to express in our theory the major distinctions by which men understand the differences in their behaviour"* (p. 178). Descriptions must, therefore, take account of persons' self-understanding (based on not-being-at-home experiences) in order not to do violence to the phenomena. This position is important because it expressly states that one cannot describe being a person without taking into account that a person has a perspective on the world and on himself/herself.

In contrast to this view, behaviourist language emphasises that it is only observable behaviour that is important to scientific knowledge. There was a strong tendency among leading behaviourist researchers (Watson, Hull, Tolman, Skinner, etc.) to regard assertions about personalised aspects of knowledge and intentional dimensions as (cognitively) meaningless and underhand descriptions of observable behaviour. The rejection of a tacit and immanent nothing can be investigated scientifically, among other things based on its alleged shortcomings as regards producing intersubjective verifiable data (i.e. in terms of explaining stimuli/cause-response/effect-connections). This is a motive that also influences modern pedagogy and psychology.

It is possible that fundamental assumptions in modern pedagogy and psychology have made it more difficult to see the potential, relevance and benefit of taking such descriptions of a tacit nothing seriously in the research context. It is hard to envisage research that is caught up in a type of knowledge that favours formal, assertion-based causal explanations and rule-based theory and that is maintained using non-personal methods, being open to the type of descriptions that are needed to understand the performance of tacit nothing aspects (more on this in Chapters 6 and 7).

The knowledge argument

The moral argument about taking account of first-person experiences and the research participants' perspective does not necessarily mean that the research participants can themselves articulate all the knowledge that is practised. Not all knowledge can be exhaustively expressed in verbal and written statements. Polanyi (2009, p. 16) writes that *we can know more than we can say*, which turns the spotlight on aspects of knowledge that qualify as knowledge, but that it is not always possible to express explicitly. This knowledge argument may sound trustworthy and innocent, but the underlying implications on which the statement is based are radical and can lead to drastic shifts of perspective for pedagogy. For reasons of space, I will not discuss the consequences of such a shift here, but we can look at some examples relating to Polanyi's statement.

There is one question that can be said to be at the core of the issue: Does theory/language fall short in terms of describing the performance of nothing? The same question is often asked about art: Does language fall short as regards describing art? If you find it difficult to answer the following questions, you will soon realise the limitations of language/theory in relation to art: How is it possible to assert the importance of experiencing Munch's introverted, petrified and life-critical *Scream* motif? Is it possible to fully express in language the value of experiencing Salvador Dali's surrealistic paintings? Is it possible to prove that Duke Ellington swings? How can Beethoven's greatness be proved? Is the experience of listening to music as good if you cannot read music? Perhaps language also falls short in relation to our way of being people. For a physiology researcher, for example, it is both true and important that the secretion of saliva increases in a systematic and orderly way when people kiss, and he would explain a kiss in terms of saliva production and hormonal fluctuations. This is a kind of know-that knowledge that can be credibly presented in tables and forms and that is important to the researcher. That part of reality is irrelevant, however, to those who are kissing (hopefully). Through expressing ourselves as people by, for example, kissing or making music, we make use of a different language and a different form of expression than the language that scientific know-that knowledge represents. We who have danced, made music or kissed should know that the analyses of know-that knowledge do not tell the whole truth. We can challenge traditional scientific knowledge by citing examples where kissing, music and art show how the truth is manifested in our own reality. How science should relate to people's intimate (and potentially uncanny nothing) praxis is a big and problematic question. Perhaps claiming to know the intimate meaning of experiences is the same as mentioning silence; if you mention it, then, in a sense, it no longer exists. These examples show that theoretical and formal knowledge is not sufficient on its own. In one sense, we have to trust in an aspect of knowledge that is (theoretically) unfounded, in the sense that it is practised without being precise, logical and explanatory. It is knowledge with a vague basis, but it is nonetheless knowledge that is "precise" in the sense it is actually practised with varying degrees of success. Perhaps the most important pedagogical task is to show how we (researchers, teachers, students, school owners, etc.) can tackle a fundamental aspect of professional and vocational development.

References
Brown, J. S., Collins, A., & Duguid, P. (1989). Situated Cognition and the Culture of Learning. *Educational Researcher*, 18(1), pp. 32–42.

Darling-Hammond, L., & Bransford, J. (2005). *Preparing Teachers for a Changing World: What Teachers Should Learn and Be Able to Do*. San Francisco: Jossey-Bass.

Dreyfus, H., & Dreyfus, S. (1986). *Mind over Machine: The Power of Human Intuition and Expertise in the Era of the Computer*. New York: The Free Press.

Engeström, Y. (1996). Developmental Work Research as Educational Research. *Nordisk Pedagogik: Journal of Nordic Educational Research*, 16, pp. 131–143.

Guerriero, S. (Ed.) (2017). *Pedagogical Knowledge and the Changing Nature of the Teaching Profession*. Paris: OECD Publishing. http://doi.org/10.1787/9789264270695-en

Lave, J., & Wenger, E. (1991). *Situated Learning: Legitimate Peripheral Participation*. Cambridge and New York: Cambridge University Press.

Polanyi, M. (2009). *The Tacit Dimension*. Chicago: The University of Chicago Press.

Resnick, L. B. (1987). The 1987 Presidential Address: Learning in School and Out. *Educational Researcher*, 16(9), pp. 13–20.

Schön, D. (1987). *Presentation to the 1987 Meeting of the American Educational Research Association*. Retrieved June 27, 2009, from http://educ.queensu.ca/~russellt/forum/schon87.htm

Taylor, C. (1985). *Human Agency and Language* (Vol. 1). Cambridge: Cambridge University Press.

Wertsch, J. V. (1991). *Voices of the Mind: A Sociocultural Approach to Mediated Action*. Cambridge, MA: Harvard University Press.

3 Technology in educational theory and practice

In educational practices and their conceptualisation, when scholars and practitioners write and talk about education and pedagogy, there is very little about nothing and much more about technology. In order to justify such a statement, I extract three illustrations pertaining to (1) preset curricular endpoints, (2) competence-based education and (3) learning theories.

Preset curricular endpoints

As part of a technological tendency, educationalists (i.e. educational practitioners and scholars of education) use technology to increase the likelihood of achieving essentially non-(nothing-)educational and non-educational means such as increasing test scores and learning outcomes (Johnson & Johnson, 1991). Moreover, "non-nothing educational means" may be defined as preset curricular endpoints, at which students have to arrive.

Apparently, it seems obvious that preset endpoints contradict the indeterminate nature of nothing (cf. Chapter 1, p. 3), in which all teachers, students and researchers are genuinely interested in topics, issues, and inquiries they discuss. The list that follows of non-nothing ends, for which technology is used, is incomplete but indicative of the purpose. In technological approaches, the notion of pedagogical nothing can be rather diverse, ranging in meaning from any competence-learning-oriented issues with at best a glimpse of nothing potential to a rather elaborate format of problem-based investigation as it is in a Socratic method. It is possible to delineate the following characteristics of a technological approach to nothing pedagogy:

1   Nothing pedagogy serves at best as an effective means for non-nothing ends, which are understood outside of the notion of nothing, within a deontological framework.
2   Nothing pedagogy is viewed as a self-contained instructional method (strategy) and activity among other (non-nothing) instructional methods

DOI: 10.4324/9781003222231-4

(strategies) and activities (e.g. "didactic instruction of factual information", see Adler, 1982), "Nothing" is a way of being treated as an activity directed towards discovery and new (self)-understanding, which
has its primer value and aims to improve the knowledge and skills
(competence) of its participants.

3   Pedagogical nothing can and should be switched on and off depending
on the instructional and educational needs.

4   Pedagogical nothing is aimed at efficient achievement of curricular
endpoints preset by the teacher and/or education policy (e.g. understanding that the definition of technology is more important than the
issue of its origin).

It may be tempting to follow such a line of distinction and isolation between
technology and nothing. In contrast, this book *emphasises* that all dominant
technological features in education and pedagogy are essentially Nothing
and thus penetrating all aspects of pedagogy and education. So, the question
should instead be, "How does the sublime nature of nothing manifest itself
in technology?" (more on this in Vignettes and examples).

Competence-based education

Another "shadow" companion with nothing is the perspective of competence. The concept of competence as an educational concept originated in
the United States and Canada in the 1960s (Hodge, 2007; Tchibozo, 2011).
The societal background was the Soviet launch and success of the satellite
"Sputnik I" into orbit around the earth in 1957, spurring educational reform
in the United States and fronting accountability and competences in behavioural terms (Hodge, 2007).

A few decades ago, competence as a concept evolved as the dream of
education (Wulf, 2003) to equip students with the ability to manage an
increasingly complex knowledge society. Although, beginning in 2012, the
OECD uses the term "skills" and not "competences" (OECD, 2012) (skills
are higher-order mental processes, for instance problem-solving, reasoning
and thinking, producing a re-ordering or extension of the existing cognitive
structure (Bloom, Engelhardt, Furst, Hill, & Krathwohl, 1956)), the learning
objectives are identical in nature, that is they are solely described in behavioural terms, in terms of learning outcomes. The dominant implementation
of competence-based education and assessment in different national contexts, as well as across the European Union, also poses a challenge (Hillen,
Sturm, & Willbergh, 2011; Leat, Thomas, & Reid, 2012; Méhaut & Winch,
2012; Nieveen, 2012; Papanastasiou, 2012; Scholl, 2012; Seikkula-Leino,
2012; Sivesind, 2013; Sundberg, 2012).

Researchers have pointed to severe challenges and problems in education caused by competence/skill-based education and assessment, such as increased teaching to the test, a narrowed curriculum, a fragmentation of educational content, reproduction of knowledge (opposed to innovative knowledge creation), increased inequality in education, increased individualisation damaging democratic education, disempowered teachers and poorer teacher–student relationships (Au, 2011; Biesta, 2010; Diamond, 2012; Edelstein, 2011; Elstad & Sivesind, 2010; Hopmann, 2007, 2008, 2013; Hopmann, Brinek, & Retzl, 2007; Hörmann, 2011; Langfeldt, Elstad, & Hopmann, 2008; Mausethagen, 2013; Tanner, 2013; Westera, 2001; Young, 2013).

Moreover, according to Standish (2012), there is a movement in education to consider learning as performance that in principle is transparent and accounted for, resulting in the construction of tests to verify that the intended learning outcomes are reached. The concept of skills is such a construct. Hence, educational problems occur as a result of implementing skills in education, when competence turns into performance, learning outcomes and skills.

Since then the term performance has become a handy catch-all for the many ways in which measures of efficient performance have come to dominate higher education institutions around the world, measures that play a key part in what we have come to call the culture of accountability (Lyotard, 1984). The central value of such a system is "*the optimization of the global relationship between input and output – in other words, performativity*" (Lyotard, 1984, p. 11). According to Lyotard (1984), accountability is perverted and turned into a technological game, where principles are no longer according to what is true, just or beautiful. The criterion now is efficiency, leading to wealth creation with the onus on technological improvement and product realisation. The question "Is it true?" is replaced by questions about efficiency and usefulness. What is taught is the "*organized stock of established knowledge, rather than knowledge defined by criteria such as truth, justice or low performativity*" (Lyotard, 1984, p. 50).

The last several waves of educational policy reform have been heavily influenced by the culture and broad umbrella of positivism (technological games, e.g. transparency, accountability and learning outcome). The proliferation of standardised testing under No Child Left Behind and the creation of a set of national standards for math and literacy under the Obama administration have been aspects of the neoliberal regime of standardisation, accountability and control. Under the logic of positivism, the teaching and learning process, a distinctly human endeavour becomes something to control and measure. It comes as no surprise, then, that technology becomes a mechanism through which such reform initiatives are implemented.

Initially, then, there seem to be reasons to modify our expectations of technological transparency, on every level where technology (and the always already potential of nothing) is present (see Chapters 6 and 7). It should modify and deepen our sense of what education and the pursuit of technology entail. It follows from the above that the present moment – me, here, now – does not exist as what I think of as the present moment without those systems that differentiate me from you/them/it/etc., and here from there, and now from later/earlier, etc. Rather than isolating and identifying the present technology as a secure point, it may turn out that presence (Being) depends on what is not (not here, not now, nothing). Hence, verificationism's account of meaning in education (which addresses the central idea about linking some sort of meaningfulness with confirmation as discussed in Carnap, 1967), among others, cannot be 100% correct.

Surprisingly, this latter-day verificationism as a kind of outdated perspective, lives on strongly today as an educational technology that may reinforce a misunderstanding of educational practice. That is to say, it invites the dominance of technical reason and effects and installs a displacement of understanding (nothing and being) and practical judgement. In fact, our being (and nothing) (what we think and do now and in the future) always operates in a way that is beyond our full control. This is so in two respects: in the first place, our way of being extends beyond anything we can know; and, in the second, whatever educational being we may be(come) cannot possibly be fully foreseen. This (positive) negativity and hiddenness and openness to possibility is at the heart of Nothing and of ourselves, and it is dynamic and transformative.

Learning theories

The non-nothing and exhaustive technological tendency is also present in theories within pedagogical learning theories. For example, when (socially) dominant cognitive learning theories with severe pedagogical implications offer the optimal pathfinding for becoming human beings such as teachers and students, it is argued that there is some form of continuity between levels and stages. Something somehow displays change; nevertheless, this something (cognition) also holds to an underlying unity and continuity. Mechanisms are set out that are used to account for developmental and learning change, difference and continuity. The account of logical-conceptual change is done through the application of the general models of development (i.e. Piaget, 1985; Vygotsky, 1987). Such mechanism is a consistent account that applies to shared practices as much as to technological artefacts and scientific ideas. One commonality is the assumption about increasing quality of development, for example systemic thinking over syncretic thinking (Vygotsky, 1987), formal-operation thinking over preoperational thinking (Piaget, 1985), theoretical over concrete (Davydov, 2008), symphonic thinking over absurdist thinking (see a description of an innovative school using this hierarchy in von Duyke, 2013), dialectical thinking over formal logical thinking (Ilyenkov, 1977), high culture over low culture and advanced culture over primitive culture (Vygotsky & Luria, 1993).

One striking parallel with Aristotelian terminology occurs here. Using Aristotelian *poiesis-praxis* terminology (Aristotle, 2000), technological-enframed education transforms a practice in poiesis, in which goal, endpoint and virtue (i.e. what is good) are (somewhat) known in advance; while Nothing (and Being) considers a practice as *praxis*, in which purpose, endpoint and virtue emerge in the activity (and passivity) itself. Because of this *poiesis* nature of practice in technology, it tends to pre-define the virtue of its intellectual endeavour in the fixed hierarchy of the binary preset "good" over the preset "bad".

References

Adler, M. J. (1982). *The Paideia Proposal: An Educational Manifesto* (1st Macmillan paperbacks ed.). New York: Macmillan.

Aristotle. (2000). *Nicomachean Ethics* (R. Crisp, Trans.). Cambridge, UK: Cambridge University Press.

Au, W. (2011). Teaching under the New Taylorism: High-stakes Testing and the Standardization of the 21st Century Curriculum. *Journal of Curriculum Studies*, 43, pp. 25–45.

Biesta, G. (2010). Why 'What Works' Still Won't Work: From Evidence-based Education to Value-based Education. *Studies in Philosophy & Education*, 29, pp. 491–503. https://doi.org/10.1007/s11217-010-9191-x

Bloom, B. S., Engelhardt, M. D., Furst, E. J., Hill, W. H., & Krathwohl, D. R. (1956). *Taxonomy of Educational Objectives: The Classification of Educational Goals*. New York: McKay.

Carnap, R. (1967). *Der logische Aufbau der Welt* (R. A. Georg, Trans., *The Logical Structure of the World*). Berkeley: University of California Press.

Davydov, V. V. (2008). *Problems of Developmental Instruction: A Theoretical and Experimental Psychological Study* (P. Moxhay, Trans.). Hauppauge, NY: Nova Science Publishers, Inc.

Diamond, J. (2012). Accountability Policy, School Organization, and Classroom Practice. Partial Recoupling and Educational Opportunity. *Education and Urban Society*, 44, pp. 151–182.

Edelstein, W. (2011). Education for Democracy: Reasons and Strategies. *European Journal of Education*, 46, pp. 127–137.

Elstad, E., & Sivesind, K. (2010). *Pisa: Sannheten om skolen?* Oslo: Universitetsforl.

Hillen, S., Sturm, T., & Willbergh, I. (2011). *Challenges Facing Contemporary Didactics: Diversity of Students and the Role of New Media in Teaching and Learning*. Münster: Waxmann.

Hodge, S. (2007). The Origins of Competency-based Training. *Australian Journal of Adult Learning*, 47, pp. 179–191.

Hopmann, S. (2007). Restrained Teaching: The Common Core of Didaktik. *European Educational Research Journal*, 6, pp. 109–124.

Hopmann, S. (2008). No Child, No School, No State Left Behind: Schooling in the Age of Accountability. *Journal of Curriculum Studies*, 40, pp. 417–456.

Hopmann, S. (2013). The End of Schooling as We Know It? *Journal of Curriculum Studies*, 45, pp. 1–3.

Hopmann, S., Brinek, G., & Retzl, M. (2007). *Pisa zufolge pisa: Hält pisa, was es verspricht?* Wien: LIT.

Hörmann, B. (2011). Capacities in Diversified Classrooms. In S. Hillen, T. Sturm, & I. Willbergh (Eds.), *Challenges Facing Contemporary Didactics: Diversity of Students and the Role of New Media in Teaching and Learning*. Münster: Waxmann.

Ilyenkov, E. V. (1977). *Dialectical Logic: Essays on Its History and Theory*. Moscow: Progress Publishers.

Johnson, D. W., & Johnson, R. T. (1991). *Learning Together and Alone: Cooperative, Competitive, and Individualistic* (3rd ed.) Englewood Cliffs, NJ: Prentice Hall.

Langfeldt, G., Elstad, E., & Hopmann, S. (2008). *Ansvarlighet i skolen: Politiske spørsmål og pedagogiske svar: Resultater fra forskningsprosjektet "achieving school accountability in practice"*. Oslo: Cappelen akademisk forl.

Leat, D., Thomas, U., & Reid, A. (2012). The Epistemological Fog in Realising Learning to Learn in European Curriculum Policies. *European Educational Research Journal*, 11, pp. 400–412.

Lyotard, J. F. (1984). The postmodern condition. Minneapolis: University of Minnesota Press.

Mausethagen, S. (2013). A Research Review of the Impact of Accountability Policies on Teachers' Workplace Relations. *Educational Research Review*, 9, pp. 16–33.

Méhaut, P., & Winch, C. (2012). The European Qualification Framework: Skills, Competences or Knowledge? *European Educational Research Journal*, 11, pp. 369–381.

Nieveen, N. (2012). Balancing Curriculum Freedom and Regulation in the Netherlands. *European Educational Research Journal*, 11, pp. 357–368.

OECD. (2012). *Better Skills. Better Jobs. Better Lives. A Strategic Approach to Skills Policies*. Retrieved June 9, 2021, from http://skills.Oecd.Org/documents/oecdskillsstrategyfinaleng.Pdf

Papanastasiou, N. (2012). 'Europe' as an Alibi: An Overview of Twenty Years of Policy, Curricula and Textbooks in the Republic of Cyprus – and their Review. *European Educational Research Journal*, 11, pp. 413–427.

Piaget, J. (1985). *The Equilibration of Cognitive Structures: The Central Problem of Intellectual Development*. Chicago: University of Chicago Press.

Scholl, D. (2012). Are the Traditional Curricula Dispensable? A Feature Pattern to Compare Different Types of Curriculum and a Critical View of Educational Standards and Essential Curricula in Germany. *European Educational Research Journal*, 11, pp. 328–341.

Seikkula-Leino, J. (2012). Facing the Changing Demands of Europe: Integrating Entrepreneurship Education in Finnish Teacher Training Curricula. *European Educational Research Journal*, 11, pp. 382–399.

Sivesind, K. (2013). Mixed Images and Merging Semantics in European Curricula. *Journal of Curriculum Studies*, 45, pp. 52–66.

Standish, P. (2012). 'This' is Produced by a 'Brain-Process'! Wittgenstein, Transparency and Psychology Today. *Journal of Philosophy of Education*, 46, pp. 61–72.

Sundberg, D. (2012). Standards-based Curricula in a Denationalised Conception of Education: The Case of Sweden. *European Educational Research Journal (EERJ)*, 11, pp. 342–355.

Tanner, D. (2013). Race to the Top and Leave the Children Behind. *Journal of Curriculum Studies*, 45, pp. 4–15.

Tchibozo, G. (2011). Emergence and Outlook of Competence-based Education in European Education Systems: An Overview. *Education, Knowledge and Economy*, 4, pp. 193–201.

von Duyke, K. (2013). *Students' Agency, Autonomy, and Emergent Learning Interests in Two Open Democratic Schools*. PhD, University of Delaware.

Vygotsky, L. S. (1987). *The Collected Works of L.S. Vygotsky: Volume 1: Thinking and Speech* (N. Minick, Trans., Vol. 1). New York: Plenum Press.

Vygotsky, L. S., & Luria, A. R. (1993). *Studies on the History of Behavior: Ape, Primitive, and Child*. Hillsdale, NJ: Lawrence Erlbaum Associates.

Westera, W. (2001). Competences in Education: A Confusion of Tongues. *Journal of Curriculum Studies*, 33, pp. 75–88.

Wulf, C. (2003). The Dream of Education. *Journal of Curriculum Studies*, 35, pp. 263–274.

Young, M. (2013). Overcoming the Crisis in Curriculum Theory: A Knowledge-based Approach. *Journal of Curriculum Studies*, 45, pp. 101–118.

4 Heidegger and Wittgenstein on education

There are two questions being asked here. Firstly, we pose the empirical question having to do with the impact Wittgenstein and Heidegger have in fact had on education? Secondly, how to invite speculation about or assessment of the ways in which Wittgenstein and Heidegger's thinking might have a bearing on the matter – that is, on philosophical enquiry into the nature, purposes and problems of education. For several reasons, it seems quite clear that the second question is the one that is least explored and having the most potential, since it's hard to find many direct historical-empirical links and influences between theories (Wittgenstein and Heidegger's) and educational practice.

On Heidegger and education

More than a decade ago, Michael Peters (2009) commented in an editorial dedicated to the significance of Heidegger's phenomenology for educational philosophy:

> *Heidegger and his forms of phenomenology have been a neglected figure in the field of philosophy of education in the English-speaking world. Little has been written on Heidegger or about his work and its significance for educational thought and practice.*

(p. 1)

Without doubt this has changed in recent years, with Heidegger's phenomenology having been drawn on by Gloria Dall'Alba in the discussion of "professional ways of being" (Dall'Alba, 2009), Angus Brook in the account of coming to terms with becoming a teacher (Brook, 2009), Vasco D'Agnese in his discussion of truth as disclosure via education (D'Agnese, 2015) and of the ethics of teaching (D'Agnese, 2016; see also Lewis, 2017), Yun's analysis of time as a resource in education, as well as education as

DOI: 10.4324/9781003222231-5

an existential event (Yun, 2018), and in discussions of the different possibilities of thinking in education (Bonnett, 1994; Lewin, 2015; Peters, 2007; Standish, 1992; Siegel, 2017; Williams, 2015).

In general, several scholars (i.e. Thomas & Thomson, 2015; Biesta, 2016; Thomson, 2001) draw attention to the fact that the very idea of education is thrown into question by Heidegger's critiques of instrumental thinking and what he calls humanism. Humanism is characterised as a coupling of standard conceptions of human beings, with the purpose of shaping humans in accordance with those conceptions. In Heidegger's (1998) letter on humanism, the inherent logic is that if the conceptions promoted by humanism (although in different forms, but same essence or will to power) have serious deficiencies, then associated educational (building) programmes will simply serve as vehicles for deforming learners (including students, teachers, principals, policy makers). That is to say, an enframing (technological) and instrumental way of being appears to have become the sole purpose and rationale of modern education. This enframing, or technology, seeks to reduce everything to resources (as standing-reserve), including human beings, and threatens to block off alternative possibilities of Being. This invokes a state of homelessness (nothing), in which the man loses his shelter, being, and thus becomes a stranger to his thought to himself. Moreover, existing learning theories, approaches to teaching and curriculum models are also challenged by Heidegger's critiques (Hodge, 2015; Biesta, 2016) and I might add are also confronted with homelessness and nothing.

Interpretations of Heidegger's philosophy suggest different ways by which to overcome technological threats reducing education to a world of beings (instead of the encounter with the Being of beings).[1] Some point out that an ontological curriculum is possible that promotes openness to Being (Hodge, 2015, pp. 85–104); still, others hold that authentic teaching can demonstrate radical openness, fostering authentic learning (Lewis, 2016). Perhaps, education, learning and teaching itself may be theorised as the process of disentanglement from non-thinking traditions and "external" forms of life. As such, it seems plausible to suggest that education can become an ontological education to nurture a thinking attuned to the disclosure of Being.

However, as Thomas and Thomson (2015, p. 97) emphasise, "*authentic education does not only mean education in the thinking of being*", since it indicates "being as entities" and not "being as such", which in turn tend to forget that their being rests on the ontological disclosure of our Da-sein or "being-here", the making-intelligible of the place in which we happen to find ourselves. Therefore, going astray in our thinking of being makes a potential errancy that tends to subordinate being to our thinking of it and so initiates and unfolds the withdrawal of being from human being (and thus from the being of all other entities (Thomas & Thomson, 2015)).

More specifically, Spinoza, Flores, and Dreyfus (1997) draw on Heidegger's philosophy when they advocate the ontological skills of theory-making that decontextualise everyday phenomena from everyday courses, and thereby promote the training of students in the methods and procedures of what might be called action research. They draw attention to "*the nature of disclosing and the spaces in which it occurs*" (Spinoza, Flores, & Dreyfus, 1997, p. 172). In their curriculum for disclosing, they imagine different sets of courses. A first set has to do with showing how Westerners developed and then unpacking an understanding of how we transform our background practices through history-making. Western ways would be brought out by contrasting them with non-Western ways. Another whole set of courses would have to do with understanding communication, not as the exchange of information but as the working out of how further to coordinate the separate practical activities of people, already to an extent coordinated by a style. In short, they are looking for and pointing at ways by which to create new disclosive spaces. Spinoza, Flores, and Dreyfus (1997) show the skills of grasping anomalies. When they propose the crucial "anomaly" skill, they also reject the notion that there could be a pre-fixed, ideal way to proceed, that is, an educational step-by-step manual for educational success or a standardised procedure. Proposing a new intellectual practice that works through examples to sensitise us both to the subtle details not immediately evident in our everyday background practices, and to the ways in which they contain anomalies, is the beginning of a whole new form of cultural, history-making activity. We are at our best, they say, when "*we become sensitive to anomalies that enable us to change the style of our culture*" (Spinoza, Flores, & Dreyfus, 1997, p. 181). I might add that educational participants can then respond to their (Nothing) activities in an *anticipatory* way, projecting new possible worlds. Maybe the feeling of Nothing is sometimes involved, that is, educational participants do not feel "at home" when anomaly is grasped.

The connection between Education and Heidegger is also developed by the traditionalism of Geisteswissenschaftliche Pädagogik that, for instance, Bollnow generally affirmed.[2] Otto F. Bollnow (1903–1991) combines Heidegger's phenomenology with linguistic-philosophical, anthropological and existential questions (Dilthey and Jaspers) along with a critical reception of existential philosophy and philosophy of life (Lebensphilosophie). Bollnow (1959) is interested in phenomena that are part of what he calls an "education of discontinuity", for example, crisis, awakening, guidance, venture, failure and encounter. However, the ontological dimension is not considered a fact of education that can be described empirically, but rather as an expression of life itself in the sense of Lebensphilosophie. That is to say, *"Lebensphilosophie focuses on life in its vitality, multiplicity and emotional irrationality, and pays special attention to its elemental contexts (e.g., the lifeworld), and (dis)continuities within the life course (e.g., birth, growth, death)"* (Brinkman & Friesen, 2018, p. 4). It is possible to see an opening of "nothing" in Lebensphilosophie, since "nothing" is also an expression of life itself and its many "discontinuities".

Moreover, in the Routledge series "New directions in the philosophy of education", J. Quay (2013) proposes a coherent theory of experience partly based on Heidegger's phenomenological approach and insights. Engaging Dewey, Heidegger and Peirce, Quay (2013) strives to expound a coherent theory of experience. The rationale, where experience is concerned, is John Dewey's pragmatism but this is only half the story. The other half is phenomenological, as crafted by Martin Heidegger. According to Quay (2013), Charles Sanders Peirce, whose philosophy draws pragmatism and phenomenology together into a partnership that enables an experiential philosophy to emerge, encompasses both. Quay (2013) suggests that education will benefit from such a coherent theory of experience by better comprehending its connection to life. In short, more than just knowing, more than just doing, education is about being; hence, it is possible to raise awareness against a de-ontologised educational tradition and practice which does not include everyday life in depth (the always already in being and nothing) as a starting point for education. Perhaps such an experiential philosophy may be conceived in terms of an awakening to (self-)responsibility that rests on an ethical "connection" between tradition and new (nothing) possibilities. This seems to be an educational conception championed by Heidegger (1998) and framed as follows:

> *The handing down in tradition is not a mere passing on, it is the preservation of what is original, it is the safeguarding of the new possibilities of the already spoken language . . . It [the language itself] lays claim to the human being to say the world anew from the language that is preserved.*
>
> (p. 142)

On such a "safeguarding of the new possibilities" background, it is possible to understand Heidegger's (1968) account of teaching and learning:

> *Teaching is even more difficult than learning. We know that; but we rarely think about it. And why is teaching more difficult than learning? Not because the teacher must have a larger store of information, and have it always ready. Teaching is more difficult than learning because what teaching calls for is this: to let learn. The real teacher, in fact, lets*

nothing else be learned than – learning. His conduct, therefore, often produces the impression that we properly learn nothing from him, if by "learning" we now suddenly understand merely the procurement of useful information. The teacher is ahead of his apprentices in this alone, that he has still far more to learn than they – he has to learn to let them learn.

(p. 15)

This may seem like a blurred or confusing statement the meaning of which initially appears difficult to decipher. But consider that *Teaching is more difficult than learning because what teaching calls for is this: to let learn.* Intuitively we think about teaching and learning as different domains partly because language lets us do so (also because of our assumptions about authority, knowledge). If we look at the German language, teaching means Lehren and learning means Lernen, and hence it is easier to see them intertwined (teaching to let learn) because of their common etymological origin. In other words, the attention and emphasis are on the students' possibilities, as they grope their way towards personal understanding and knowledge. An unsettling question arises: What is the nature of teaching that allows learning and possibilities to occur? How might we establish conditions conducive to letting learning occur and possibilities to emerge? (more on such questions in Chapter 8).

Wittgenstein on educational literature

Wittgenstein's philosophy is no less complicated, complex and multifaceted than is Heidegger's philosophy, and likewise there is no lack of possible and highly different educational implications. I would like to highlight two different educational views which are based on (interpretations of) Wittgenstein: (1) training for self-responsibility and (2) the method of deconstruction or grammatical investigation.

Firstly, it is important to mention a monumental work regarding Wittgenstein and education, namely *A Companion to Wittgenstein on Education: Philosophical Investigations*, edited by M. Peters and J. Stickney (2017). The collection comprises 50 chapters, grouped under the headings such as "Mediations on Wittgenstein and Education" (Bai, 2017), "Wittgenstein as educator" (Stickney, 2017), "Slow Learning and the Multiplicity of Meaning" (Smith, 2017) and Wittgenstein's metaphors and his pedagogical philosophy (Burbules, 2017). As quoted from the abstract of Peters and Stickney (2017):

This collection explores Wittgenstein not so much as a philosopher who provides a method for teaching or analyzing educational concepts but

> *rather as one who approaches philosophical questions from a pedagogical point of view. Wittgenstein's philosophy is essentially pedagogical: he provides pictures, drawings, analogies, similes, jokes, equations, dialogues with himself, questions and wrong answers, experiments and so on, as a means of shifting our thinking, or of helping us escape the pictures that hold us captive.*

This is an important statement for two inherently linked reasons. Firstly, because it is advisable not to look for educational theory in Wittgenstein's writing but instead to see his later philosophy as pedagogical (Peters, 1995; Peters & Marshall, 1999; Peters, Burbules, & Smeyers, 2008) or as therapeutic (Smeyers, Smith, & Standish, 2007) and not to regard pedagogy as a "science" (Standish, 1995). Secondly, there seem to be consensus (cf. Peters & Stickney, 2017) that Wittgenstein does not intend to establish a (pedagogical) theory at all when he talks about the teaching and learning of language. The theoretical attitude is rejected, for there is no use for an attitude of seeking the essence of words, generalising phenomena, and asking for explanations even when we don't need them (cf. McGinn, 1997, p. 16). So, the purpose is not compatible with advancing theory and empirical investigations,[3] and, more importantly, it is an argument against the idea that everything can be explained by science.

Even though using Wittgenstein's philosophy in terms of empirical research may be a contradiction in terms (cf. the intention of not advancing any theory of "hidden processes"), this is not an argument against acknowledging the practical relevance and implications of his philosophy. Bakhurst (2017) asks to what extent Wittgenstein helps in this respect? His answer is by examples (rule following) and existential drama. Let's look more closely at the theme of existential drama. There is the "existential drama" in Wittgenstein's philosophical writing and its manner of drawing the reader into the "*movement of his thought – the unstinting struggling, questioning, doubting, proposing, conjecturing, agonizing – in a way that is profoundly authentic and unaffected*" (Bakhurst, 2017, p. xi). This indicates that (educational) philosophy is primarily a specific activity which offers no theory of education but nevertheless has practical significance. So, what does this activity consist of? "*It involves working upon oneself to quieten conceptual anxieties so that we see things aright (CV 16) and liberate ourselves from debilitating perplexity*" (Bakhurst, 2017, p. vi). This is something else than the applicable modus operandi of many educational philosophers (i.e. the endeavour to solve practical problems concerning learning, teaching, curricula, policy, etc.). Instead the Wittgensteinian approach puts into question the very conceptions of knowledge, reason and self that are central to education as modernity understands it.

Training for self-responsibility

Throughout Wittgenstein's work in philosophy, it seems important for him to be someone with *something to say* and to be able to *explain* what he means. This is inseparable from the handing down of the *use* of words in a language, so that there is a deep connection between "*the concept of teaching and the concept of meaning*" (Wittgenstein, 1967, §412). Moreover, *teaching* here is not merely instruction but also *training*: "any explanation has its foundation in training", he stressed, adding parenthetically "(Educators ought to remember this.)" (Wittgenstein, 1967, §419). This means that training is the avenue leading us into the performance of language games (Stickney, 2017).

When Wittgenstein (1958) spoke of children being "trained" he was using this word, he said, "*in a way strictly analogous to the way in which we speak of an animal being trained*" (p. 77). The underlying claim is that in learning a language, the child "learns to react in such-and-such a way". It involves learning responses and behaviour. As with trained animals, children begin from a place of trust. With time, they develop the abilities and dispositions necessary for membership in a linguistic community. This occurs through their immersion in language games that are constituted as social. Furthermore, who we become is thus a profoundly intergenerational affair, a "handing down" in tradition, and has its foundation in a training regime through which one acquires new possibilities of being, acting and speaking.

With regard to his own teaching experience, Wittgenstein (1993, p. 19) explicitly says that he was attempting to "awaken" an "orthographic conscience". Teaching spelling should not, Wittgenstein stressed in his preface to the dictionary, be interested in "average spelling" results: "It is not *the class* that should learn to spell but each *individual* student", and this requires that the individual student develops a strong sense of responsibility for their own spelling (Wittgenstein, 1993, p. 15). As Hilmy points out (1987, p. 5), such remarks echo the point emphasised in the Preface to the *Investigations*, "*I should not like my writing to spare other people the trouble of thinking. But, if possible, to stimulate someone to thoughts of his own.*" Therefore, it seems reasonable to suggest that the educational task is to cultivate such "awakening" in students. Furthermore, the task here belongs to a practical teaching tradition aimed, quite generally, at cultivating *intense self-responsibility* in each individual student: "*He should feel that he is the only author of his work and he alone should be responsible for it*" (Wittgenstein, 1993, p. 15).

This is the basic question of how one comes to live a good life and how one comes to know. In other words, questions of education, of teaching and of learning are already there at the heart of philosophy, as Wittgenstein's (1953) work amply attests.

Grammatical concerns

It should be clear that Wittgenstein does not intend to contribute to building a theory for empirical (educational) research when he discusses how words are taught. The better word for describing the project is grammatical.

Wittgenstein (1953) himself calls his approach "grammatical investigation". Such an investigation sheds light on our problem by clearing misunderstandings away. It is important to recognise that Wittgenstein's use of the concept of grammar at least in two ways is different from the traditional one. As McGinn (1984) points out, firstly, "grammar" considers language not as a system of signs but as human activities with words, or our practice of using language. Secondly, grammatical investigation deals not with phenomena but with the possibility of phenomena, by examining our use of language.

Wittgenstein's (1953) discussion of teaching, which brings about concept clarification, serves as a grammatical investigation. However, this is an entirely new *kind* of method, *and "learning it requires breaking the linguistic habits of a lifetime and acquiring new ones"* (Staten, 1984, p. 66). It is *"a blind and mute method, taught only by being practiced"*, or *"the method of destabilization"* (Staten, 1984, p. 66 and 75) dissolving, destruction. It seems obvious that the method is difficult in the extreme to teach or to learn because it demands a new way of being and thinking, that is to say, not in that it provides knowledge (Wissen), but rather in that it stimulates thinking (Denken).

A passage from the *Investigations* may provide an indication of the method:

> *Look at a stone and imagine it having sensations. -One says to oneself: How could one so much as get the idea of ascribing a sensation to a thing? One might as well ascribe it to a number! -And now look at a wriggling fly and at once these difficulties vanish and pain seems able to get a foothold here, where before everything was, so to speak, too smooth for it.*
>
> (Wittgenstein, 1953, p. 284)

Here, the essential is the skill of making sense of what at first sight appears not to make sense. It is the skill that allows us to attain something strange from something with which we are familiar. The innovation is that the current use of our words, a medium in which we are held captive, can be overcome when we encounter a new use.

In summary

In order to draw out the significance of what is at stake here, I shall briefly identify two "drives" that operate through the literature involving Heidegger and Wittgenstein's philosophical tenets on education. I shall then relate these to the guiding concept of *nothing* discussed in this book.

1   Wittgenstein and Heidegger insisted (although for different reasons) that the traditional epistemological concerns were misguided because they cannot be answered; hence, educational practice cannot trust, and cannot be solely based on, an epistemological foundation. This may open the road of Nothingness in terms of praxis.

2   The Existence (being-nothing), that finds itself thrown into the world amidst things and with others, is thrown into its *possibilities* (cf. Chapter 5). The individual needs to assume these possibilities in order to assess the innermost individuality of the world. If not, we may lose the primeval openness of Existence towards Being. We merely achieve the despicable openness to the "will to power", and given the overwhelming dominance of the technological imperative, of instrumental reason, and of what has come to be called "performativity" in prevailing philosophies and practices of education, it may be needed to revitalise the meaning of Being and Nothing.

Notes

1   In other words, Heidegger (1999, p. 4) states that *"The time of 'systems is over. The time of re-building the essential shaping of beings according to the truth of being has not yet arrived . . . How is this one thing to be accomplished."*

2   As Brinkmann (2016, pp. 2–3) notes in a historical review,

> *In the 1960s and 1970s, German scholars suggested concepts which develop the phenomenological approach further and stand in critical differentiation from Bollnow's anthropological Phenomenological Theory of Bildung and Education and hermeneutical pedagogy. Gunther Buck, Heinrich Rombach, Werner Loch, Eugen Fink, and Egon Schutz refer to Husserl, Heidegger, and Gadamer and are able to develop genuinely phenomenological approaches for a theory of learning, Bildung, and education.*

3   However, this does not mean that Wittgenstein denies the value of empirical research, or that empirical researchers cannot learn anything from Wittgenstein. What is wrong is to claim that Wittgenstein is involved in establishing a theory for

empirical study. The applicability of Wittgenstein's philosophy and the intention of his philosophy may be and often are different.

References

Bai, H. (2017). Meditation on Wittgenstein and Education. In M. Peters & J. Stickney (Eds.), *A Companion to Wittgenstein on Education: Philosophical Investigations* (pp. 401–415). Singapore: Springer Nature.

Bakhurst, D. (2017). Foreword. In M. Peters & J. Stickney (Eds.), *A Companion to Wittgenstein on Education: Philosophical Investigations* (pp. v–xii). Singapore: Springer Nature.

Biesta, G. J. J. (2016). Who's Afraid of Teaching? Heidegger and the Question of Education ('Bildung'/'Erziehung'). *Educational Philosophy and Theory*, 48(8), pp. 832–845.

Bollnow, O. F. (1959). *Existenzphilosophie und Pädagogik. Versuch über unstetige Formen der Erziehung.* Stuttgart, Germany: Kohlhammer.

Bonnett, M. (1994). *Children's Thinking: Promoting Understanding in the Primary School.* New York: Cassell Education Ltd.

Brinkmann, M. (2016). Phenomenological Theory of Bildung and Education. In M. A. Peters (Ed.), *Encyclopedia of Educational Philosophy and Theory.* Springer: Singapore. https://doi.org/10.1007/978-981-287-532-7_94-1

Brinkmann, M., & Friesen, N. (2018). Phenomenology and Education. In *International Handbook of Philosophy of Education* (pp. 1–16). https://doi.org/10.1007/978-3-319-72761-5

Brook, A. (2009). The Potentiality of Authenticity in Becoming a Teacher. In G. Dall'Alba (Ed.), *Exploring Education through Phenomenology* (pp. 53–65). Oxford: Wiley Blackwell.

Burbules, N. (2017). Wittgenstein's Metaphors and His Pedagogical Philosophy. In M. Peters & J. Stickney (Eds.), *A Companion to Wittgenstein on Education: Philosophical Investigations* (pp. 123–133). Singapore: Springer Nature.

D'Agnese, V. (2015). The Inner Violence of Reason: Re-reading Heidegger via Education *Journal of Philosophy of Education*, 49(3), pp. 435–455.

D'Agnese, V. (2016). Facing Paradox Everyday: A Heideggerian Approach to the Ethics of Teaching. *Ethics and Education*, 11(2), pp. 159–174.

Dall'Alba, G. (2009). *Exploring Education Through Phenomenology: Diverse Approaches.* Hoboken, NJ: Wiley-Blackwell.

Heidegger, M. (1968). *What is Called Thinking?* (F. D. Wieck & J. G. Gray, Trans.). New York: Harper Collins.

Heidegger, M. (1998). Letter on Humanism. In W. McNeil (Ed.), *Pathmarks.* Cambridge: Cambridge University Press.

Heidegger, M. (1999). On the Essence of Truth. In *Martin Heidegger: Pathmarks.* New York: Cambridge: Cambridge University Press.

Hilmy, S. S. (1987). *The Later Wittgenstein: The Emergence of a New Philosophical Method.* Oxford: Blackwell.

Hodge, S. (2015). *Challenge to Education*. Springer International Publishing.

Lewin, D. (2015). Heidegger East and West: Philosophy as Educative Contemplation. *Journal of Philosophy of Education*, 49(2), pp. 221–239.

Lewis, T. E. (2017). Study Time: Heidegger and the Temporality of Education. *Journal of Philosophy of Education*, 51(1), pp. 230–247.

McGinn, C. (1984). *Wittgenstein on Meaning*. Oxford: Blackwell.

McGinn, M. (1997).*Wittgenstein and the Philosophical Investigations*. London: Routledge.

Peters, M. A. (1995). Philosophy and Education: 'After' Wittgenstein. In J. Marshall & P. Smeyers (Eds.), *Philosophy and Education: Accepting Wittgenstein's Challenge* (pp. 189–204). Dordrecht, Boston and London: Kluwer Academic Publishers.

Peters, M. A. (2007). Kinds of Thinking, Styles of Reasoning. *Educational Philosophy and Theory*, 39(4), pp. 350–364.

Peters, M. A. (2009). Editorial: Heidegger, Phenomenology, Education. *Educational Philosophy and Theory*, 41(1), pp. 1–6. https://doi.org/10.1111/j.1469-5812.2008.00516.x

Peters, M. A., Burbules, N., & Smeyers, P. (2008). *Showing and Doing: Wittgenstein as a Pedagogical Philosopher*. Boulder, CO: Paradigm Publishers.

Peters, M. A., & Marshall, J. (1999). *Wittgenstein: Philosophy, Postmodernism, Pedagogy*. Westport, CT and London: Bergin and Garvey.

Peters, M., & Stickney, J. (Eds.) (2017). *A Companion to Wittgenstein on Education: Philosophical Investigations*. Singapore: Springer Nature.

Quay, J. (2013). *Education, Experience and Existence: Engaging Dewey, Peirce and Heidegger*. London: Routledge.

Siegel, H. (2017). Epistemology in Excess: A Response to Williams. *Journal of Philosophy of Education*, 51(1), pp. 193–213.

Smeyers, P., Smith, R., & Standish, P. (2007). *The Therapy of Education: Philosophy, Happiness and Personal Growth*. London: Palgrave Macmillan.

Smith, R. (2017). Slow Learning and the Multiplicity of Meaning. In M. Peters & J. Stickney (Eds.), *A Companion to Wittgenstein on Education: Philosophical Investigations* (pp. 101–113). Singapore: Springer Nature.

Spinoza, C., Flores, F., & Dreyfus, H. (1997). *Disclosing New Worlds: Democratic Action and the Cultivation of Solidarity*. Cambridge, MA: MIT Press.

Standish, P. (1992). *Beyond the Self: Wittgenstein, Heidegger and the Limits of Language*. Aldershot: Ashgate Publishing Group.

Standish, P. (1995). Why We Should Not Speak of an Educational Science. In P. Smeyers & J. D. Marshall (Eds.), *Philosophy and Education: Accepting Wittgenstein's Challenge* (pp. 143–157). Dordrecht: Kluwer.

Staten, H. (1984). *Wittgenstein and Derrida*. Lincoln: University of Nebraska Press.

Stickney, J. (2017). Wittgenstein as Educator. In M. Peters & J. Stickney (Eds.), *A Companion to Wittgenstein on Education: Philosophical Investigations* (pp. 43–61). Singapore: Springer Nature.

Thomas, C., & Thomson, I. (2015). Heidegger's Contributions to education (from thinking). *Chiasma: A Site for Thought*, 2, pp. 96–108.

Thomson, I. D. (2001). Heidegger on Ontological Education, Or: How We Become What We Are. *Inquiry*, 44(3), pp. 243–268. https://doi.org/10.1080/0020174013169224408

Williams, E. (2015). In Excess of Epistemology: Siegel, Taylor, Heidegger and the Conditions of Thought. *Journal of Philosophy of Education*, 49(1), pp. 142–160.

Wittgenstein, L. (1953). *Philosophische Untersuchungen* (Translated as *Philosophical Investigations* [in German and English], Rev. 4th ed., by G. E. M. Anscombe, P. M. S. Hacker, & J. Schulte). Chichester, West Sussex, UK and Malden, MA: Wiley-Blackwell, 2009.

Wittgenstein, L. (1958). *The Blue and Brown Books*. Oxford: Blackwell.

Wittgenstein, L. (1967). *Zettel* (G. E. M. Anscombe & G. H. von Wright, Eds.). Oxford: Blackwell.

Wittgenstein, L. (1993). *Philosophical Occasions: 1912–1951*. Indianapolis, IN: Hackett Publishing.

Yun, S. (2018). Heidegger and the Recovery of Education. In *International Handbook of Philosophy of Education* (pp. 211–224). Switzerland: Springer. https://doi.org/10.1007/978-3-319-72761-5_18

5 Heidegger and Wittgenstein combined towards a theory of nothing

The argument in this part is that a short comparative study of Wittgenstein and Heidegger's engagement with the decline of the technological age, phenomenology and language may result in some new thought on a "theory"[1] of nothing in educational practice. At first glance, it may be difficult to imagine two philosophers who have less in common than L. Wittgenstein and M. Heidegger. It can be argued that this owes to the barriers of the "Analytical-Continental" divide.[2] Consider, for instance, their starting points. Whereas Wittgenstein started from a logical frame of reference where the logic of assertions was to be analysed to ascertain the basic structure of the world, Heidegger started from a purely phenomenological frame of reference, that is to say, human experience was to be explored for the light it could cast on the nature of Being. However, one parallel can be found in their "later" philosophy in the assumption that it is impossible to find a language that will mirror the world. Though they certainly differed in their terminology, both came to the insight that what is most important in life cannot be (clearly) said at all (for Wittgenstein, merely shown, and for Heidegger, left to nothing or poetry). Both also highlighted an important realisation; namely, that what cannot be said is the relation between language and reality. Another parallel is the rebellion against the whole enterprise of philosophy as they had originally conceived it, that is Wittgenstein wanted to cure us of our hinges for saying the unsayable; Heidegger wanted to leave us open to the awaiting and call of Being. Moreover, their starting points perhaps also converge on a deeper level and are not so different.

Going deeper, my central argument is that by approaching some of Wittgenstein's philosophy in "a lost-man way", it is possible to make a more sense of the equivalence, because the very same (phenomenological) problem-set, I suggest, can be found in Heidegger's remarks on Nothing. Moreover, the assumption that Wittgenstein and Heidegger both came to view language itself as the pre-educational nothing, characterised as wordlessness and non-identity, presents a way beyond the word and technological

DOI: 10.4324/9781003222231-6

world views. In outlying the shared strains of their respective disclosures on the relation between language and the world of education, it is possible to show something *yet unsaid and indicate the unsayable*, addressing our technological educational age, thinking about that which, as the *difference* between the outspoken language of technology and that which is, prepares the way towards an experience of the hitherto "impossible" meaning of non-being and nothing. In Chapter 6, many of their key concepts, such as technology and equipmentality (Heidegger), forms of life and language game (Wittgenstein), are outlined and developed as a direct response to the limits of language. In this section, the purpose is not, of course, to conduct a *comprehensive* inquiry and comparison between Heidegger and Wittgenstein on the phenomenon of nothing (which would require many books and dissertations) but to indicate some interesting parallels and resemblances with regard to phenomenological lenses and Nothing. This may serve as a window for a more detailed framework in Chapter 6. However, by looking at the ways their common ground and perspectives on phenomenology overcome such linguistic (and technological) constraints, I suggest that the phenomenological relevance of nothing (Angst) can be illuminated.

Firstly, however, with Wittgenstein as with Heidegger, the criticism and abandonment of traditional philosophy are a move away from the reductive understanding of our experience that is part of our Cartesian heritage with its emphasis on reflection and detached observation rather than doing. Of course, Heidegger and Wittgenstein claim to have done much more than going beyond Descartes (cf. Greek tragedy and the need for a philosophical dead-end and moratorium), but for the phenomenological structure of the theory of nothing, I find it unnecessary to follow them much beyond Descartes.

Thus, one main similarity between Heidegger and Wittgenstein is found in what one might call a negativity towards the 2500-year-old tradition of asking (impossible) epistemological questions understood as the search for ultimate Truth. Some scholars, especially within the analytical tradition, interpret this a-epistemological turn as a form of pragmatism (i.e. Okrent, 1988, 2013). I find this partly wrong; it is instead an ethical turn, even though neither Heidegger nor Wittgenstein explicitly focuses to any great extent on ethical issues. However, even though epistemological questions are considered a dead-end, different questions should be asked. The questions that replace epistemological fixation might be, for example, "What does it mean to be and unfold your essence? *How and when does meaning (dis)appear, and how do we apprehend meaning to its environment?*" In the final analysis, these are questions about education and as such are significant for educational practice because they enable teachers, students and researchers to engage in a form of ontological and critical thinking (which is further discussed in Chapters 7 and 8), that creates the possibility for elevating one's consciousness or way of being above tradition, and I might add educational technology such as frameworks of competence and learning (cf. Chapter 3).

On the decline of the technological age

There are possibilities for a broader and at the same time more basic perspective on Wittgenstein's philosophy through illuminating a general scepticism towards the modern belief in progress of his contemporary era. Something important to note here is that philosophical activity should not move towards the shaping of specifically new political and cultural forms of expression; *"we must only point out and resolve the injustices of philosophy, and not posit new parties – and creeds"* (Wittgenstein, quoted in Crary, 2001, p. 119). This does not mean, however, that the dis(solution) of philosophical "injustices" is not motivated out of the contemporary climate of modernity. Von Wright (1993) claims that Wittgenstein stands in opposition to a modern *"euphoric belief in progress"* and its *"managerial uses of reason in industrialised democratic societies"* (p. 101). A modern climate that underpins the opportunity to grant larger narratives, assertions/metalanguage and belief in progress privileged access to describing diverse cultural practices and affiliations between them seems to be reflected, and meets strong resistance, in Wittgenstein's philosophy. One glimpses in Wittgenstein an underlying cultural pessimism or a type of decline-of-the-West thinking. Von Wright (1982) stresses this further by claiming that Wittgenstein professed an adherence to a Spenglerian, pessimistic attitude towards the present: *"he lived the 'Untergang des Abendlandes', the decline of the West"* (p. 116). A *"rejection of scientific-technological civilisation of industrialised societies, which he regarded as the decay of a culture"* has also been attributed to Wittgenstein (Von Wright, 1982, p. 118). Von Wright's interpretation of a Western decline in Wittgenstein is currently an item of controversy, but it does at any rate point to one aspect of Wittgenstein's philosophy that renders it understandable based on a somewhat more specific societal context. In terms of Heidegger's works, the concept of decline is also present, although in another sense.

Heidegger's thoughts about deconstructing a Western metaphysics embody a wish to free himself of all traditional assumptions, terms and conceptions that might undermine the overriding issue of the meaning of Being. This means that the fundamental ontological criteria in *Sein und Zeit* rest on a type of generality that does not make them suitable for characterisation based on predetermined societal conditions. The statement *"Höher als die Wirklichkeit steht die Möglichkeit"* (Heidegger, 1960, §31) perhaps denotes the practice of opportunities rather than a strategy by which to ground philosophy in specific contemporary contexts. This does not mean, however, that the philosophy of being can divest itself of the "history of being" or its contemporary era. In the essay "The Question Concerning Technology," Heidegger (1977) uses the term *Bestand* (standing-reserve) to describe the contemporary time's technological means of covering being:

> *Everywhere everything is ordered to stand by, to be immediately at hand, indeed to stand there just so that it may be on call for a further ordering. Whatever is ordered about in this way has its own standing. We call it the standing-reserve [Bestand].*
>
> (p. 17)

What is essential here is that Heidegger (1977) points out that our dealings with technology cause what is ordered to have value/status only through the fact that it can be ordered. A type of techno-nihilism such as this denotes a modern "decline" in the sense of an existence that has a strong tendency to rely on technical devices in order thereby to sever contact with more authentic aspects of existence. It would appear as if Heidegger fears a future in which humans will have gained complete control over themselves and nature, because openness to Being may disappear. The great horror is undoubtedly that we may become, or are, so enslaved by technology that we are no longer even curious about whether there are other, richer ways by which Being can become visible. The description of technological "decline", therefore, has a normative side that, according to Heidegger (1969), does not have to "*affect our inner and real core. We can affirm the unavoidable use of technical devices, and also deny them the right to dominate us*" (p. 54). In a way, Being cannot escape its contemporary history because it is only there that it can await the dawn. This may also be interpreted as technology being surpassable only based on itself (its own essence), because replacing one will would result in an even worse form of purposeless nihilism of the will.

This, then, was a brief survey of how Wittgenstein and Heidegger's projects can be inscribed in a contemporaneity. It is impossible to see similarities in decline-oriented thinking despite their, to some extent, different descriptions of the contemporary time. Similarity emerges as something that we must be confronted with if one wishes to be honest about what happens to modern people. The two appear to be motivated by a type of historical necessity aimed at dealing with knowledge/philosophy/society and finally with their own self-understanding. This can be articulated as an ethical concern for what knowledge/philosophy/society might corrupt in terms of our self-understanding. The ethical dimension, based on a reading of both Wittgenstein and Heidegger, can be embodied in a strong concern with respect to the absence of a critical contemporary discourse and dominance of (metaphysically) objective concepts that make science immune in relation to practice. It is a matter of a decline in the era in which we live. A decline that, in line with the purpose of this book, no longer sees the meaning of an inner similarity and interdependence between technology (theory) and Nothing (practice). Wittgenstein and Heidegger share thoughts related to a decline, but undoubtedly more significant are the similarities they share in conjunction with phenomenology.

On phenomenology

To understand the potential that phenomenology holds for Heidegger and Wittgenstein[3] is not to ask whether Wittgenstein and Heidegger *are* phenomenologists or not, as was done in much of the early literature (Reeder, 1989; Gier, 1981, 1990). It is possible to delineate how Heidegger and Wittgenstein initially derived the groundless ground (Nothing) through phenomenology (a much more comprehensive, detailed and nuanced elaboration of such an issue can be found in Fay, 1992; O'Rourke, 2018). Following Fay (1992, p. 21), four "shared" elements can be found in relation to phenomenology:

1   a study of phenomena given in experience
2   a description, not an explanation
3   a key phenomenological approach "away from theory – to the things themselves"
4   a grasp and description of essential features or the essence (Wesen, Wesensschau) of experience

In order to underscore an insight that in my view implicitly penetrates all four elements, I would like to add a fifth element:

5   It is important to acquire direct insight into the full range of the phenomena's possibilities or the (im)possible possibilities (logical structure in Wittgensteinian language; Heidegger would call it Being's possibilities, defined as Dasein/Being-there).

However, with regard to the "context" of phenomena, Heidegger (1962) and (the later) Wittgenstein (2001) agree that the basis of intelligibility, the groundless ground of our conceptual apparatus, is the everyday life and shared reality in which we always already find ourselves. Hence, this mutual insight led both to prioritise description over explanation and the insight that there are meaningful forms of (philosophical) expression (based on "the things themselves") that exceed the boundaries of the logical and argument-centric (more on this issue in Chapter 8).

Herein lies the relevance of phenomenology for Heidegger and Wittgenstein (i.e. Park, 1998). With reference to Wittgenstein, Hintikka and Hintikka (1986, p. 148) postulate that

> *Wittgenstein's conception [of phenomenology] turns out to be closely similar to those of phenomenologists. Their basic idea is precisely the same . . . viz., that we can uncover the conceptual structure of the world by attending to our immediate experience.*

Wittgenstein himself also underlines this "basic idea": "*All that matters is that the signs, in no matter how complicated a way, still in the end refer to immediate experience and not to an intermediary (a thing in itself)*" (Wittgenstein, 1998, p. 282).

Hence, if Wittgenstein's view on the importance of immediate experience is deemed absurd then the entire project of the theory of nothing and the combination of Wittgenstein and Heidegger's thought in this joint effort is highly problematic. Moreover, perhaps it is possible to further connect some of Wittgenstein's philosophy to Nothing.

The style or way of philosophy as a kind of nothing-practice

Consider his formulation. A philosophical problem has the form: *I don't know my way about* (Wittgenstein, 1953, §123). For Wittgenstein, then, philosophical problems have their beginnings in the feeling of being lost and in an unfamiliar place, and philosophical answers are in the nature of finding one's way back. This image of turning back, of finding not by moving forward as towards a goal but by being-led-back or "stepping-back", is maybe pervasive in Wittgenstein's early and later writings. How can education and educational actors adopt this way of being-led-back? Is there something familiar (family resemblance) in the feeling of being lost (Nothing) in educational experience?

Wittgenstein remarks that philosophical problems have the form "*I don't know my way about.*" It is tempting to suggest that any everyday problems having this form are, therefore, with a Nothing potential, even though it can be argued that to have lost one's way in some strange city hardly suffices to make one a nothing companion in educational practice. But why not? If we are able to ask our GPS-equipped cell phone, or some local residents for help, or look for a taxi, perhaps the problem emerges against a backdrop of a more secure ways of doing things on which we can fall back in an attempt to discover where we are and where we should go.

This is an example of a man who knows his way around a city but is incapable of drawing a map (cf. Wittgenstein, 1967, §121). Every time he tries to draw a map, he gets it wrong. Here, his instinct is the only ability to find his way around the city (implying that instincts "works" without being able to say how it is played out). But imagine if the "city instinct" is not present and you are lost in the city and the only alternatives are to move around without a map and navigate on sound. Such a situation may indicate a more profound condition for your way of being and self-understanding – a condition that may imply a lost uncanny feeling, nothing or not-being-at-home experience. This is not unfamiliar to Wittgenstein. In fact, he says:

> To be sure, I can imagine what Heidegger means by being and anxiety. Man feels the urge to run up against the limits of language. . . . But this inclination, the running up against something, indicates something.
>
> (Wittgenstein & Waismann, 2003, pp. 68–69)

Wittgenstein sympathetic remark[4] on Heidegger's notions of Being and Angst implies that what Wittgenstein meant is connected with the *urge to run up against the limits of language* express the "wonder that anything at all exists" (i.e. compared to Heidegger's phrase "Why there is something rather than anything"). This also echoes remarks in the Tractatus, for example, "It is not how things are in the world that is mystical, but that it exists" (Wittgenstein, 2005, §6.44). This common theme of wonder seems important, and I might add, philosophy remains philosophy only if it retains that sense of wonder and nothing in which it has its origin. To assert that nothing cannot be replaced by technology or any other interpretative discipline is to assert that we dwell in the world without final security. Again, we are led back to Wittgenstein's thesis that philosophical problems take the form of "I have lost my way". But we must beware of separating too categorically knowing one's way and having lost one's way (more on this in Chapter 8). As soon as what is to be done becomes in any way problematic, man has thereby lost his way. Losing or not knowing his way around also enables a sort of potential or possibility, because freedom is possible only for a being uncertain of her way.

Let us recall, for Heidegger (1962), that Nothing (Angst) is what first discloses the joint structure of Dasein (Being-there) and being-in-the-world as such. Angst (Nothing) is a kind of discomfort towards the world as a whole, "*the world as such is that in the face of which one has Angst,*" according to Heidegger (1962, p. 231), and this is close to the experience that Wittgenstein (2005) captures in the phrase *"astonishment that anything exists"* (p. 68). I suggest that the Nothing (intertwined with the experienced "peculiarity" that there is something/being), the proper "object" of Nothing, is the same for both men. It resides in the meeting of language (and thought) and world as two inseparable components of which the "sum product" is the world as experienced.

However, not knowing one's way may imply that (Nothing) problems have no secure background. They emerge only where academic partici-pants (i.e. students, teachers and researchers) begin to question and are questioned by the place (background) assigned by culture, history, lan-guage, and, searching for "I know my way around" ground, while await-ing a more secure establishment of that place. Translated into educational practice, the fundamental question is "where is man's proper place?" Education comes to an end when this question is no longer raised, because man either has become secure in knowledge and faith or has found it a treacherous question to which there is no answer. If a desire for security leads human beings to education, that same desire can also lead them to forsake it.

Notes

1 In his *Remarks on Colour*, Wittgenstein (1977) claimed: *"There is no such thing as phenomenology, but there are indeed phenomenological problems"* (§53). The rejection of "phenomenology" is understandable in light of Wittgenstein's signa-ture view that the philosopher "must not advance any kind of theory" (including phenomenology) and instead that everything must be "open to view". This strong rejection of theory is based on a reading and attribution of theories concerning hidden (reality) processes. What is acceptable to infer is that the "arising"/clear-ing of language from everyday life may be of the sort that is already "open to view" – that is, a "phenomenological-problem" approach of "theory" of nothing is possible.

2 From different traditions there are different comparisons addressed between Witt-genstein and Heidegger (e.g. Mulhall, 1990, 2001; Glendinning, 1998; Romano, 2008; Braver, 2012; Egan, Reynolds, & Wendland, 2013; Apel, 1973). We must not forget the rich and influential American reception of the phenomenological tradition and its attempt to compare Husserl, Sartre, Merleau-Ponty and above all Heidegger's views with Wittgenstein's positions (see, e.g., Dreyfus, 1991; Rorty, 1991; Taylor, 1985; Brandom, 2002; Haugeland, 2013; Crowell, 2013). However, in this section, space does not permit an elaboration of each and every one of these references.

3 L. Wittgenstein used the word phenomenology twice to describe his philosophy. He used the term first in his notes from 1929, which later served as material for the posthumously published Philosophische Bemerkungen, and then again in 1951 in a collection of notes published as Bemerkungen über die Farben.

4 There are different opinions on this issue. The common view holds that Witt-genstein's position on Heidegger is essentially the same as Carnap's (cf. Richter

2007). This, of course, presumes that Carnap is actually characterising Heidegger's statements of nothing as complete nonsense (there are those who claim
that this is not the case, e.g. Stone (2006)). However, some argue that Wittgenstein does not put forward a critique at all but instead attempts to engage with
what Heidegger might mean by Nothing and "Nothing noths". Through discussion of the contributions to the debate concerning this remark from P.M.S.
Hacker (2003), G. Baker (2004), J. Conant (2001) and D. Richter (2007), I rely
on some "borrowed" arguments; namely, that we should not read Wittgenstein
as putting forward a Carnapian attack against Heidegger, and hence it may be
easier to see some major resemblances between Heidegger and Wittgenstein on
Nothing.

References

Apel, K. O. (1973). *Tranformation der Philosophie*. Frankfurt-am-Main: Suhrkamp.

Baker, G. P. (2004). Wittgenstein's Method and Psychoanalysis. In K. J. Morris (Ed.), *Wittgenstein's Method: Neglected Aspects: Essays on Wittgenstein* (pp. 205–222). Oxford: Blackwell.

Brandom, R. (2002). *Tales of the Mighty Dead. Historical Essays in the Metaphysics of Intentionality*. Cambridge, MA: Harvard University Press.

Braver, L. (2012). *Groundless Grounds: A Study of Wittgenstein and Heidegger*. Cambridge, MA: MIT Press.

Conant, J. (2001). Two Conceptions of Die Überwindung der Metaphysik: Carnap and Early Wittgenstein. In T. McCarthy & S. C. Stidd (Eds.), *Wittgenstein in America* (pp. 13–61). Oxford: Oxford University Press.

Crary, A. (2001). Wittgenstein's Philosophy in Relation to Political Thought. In I. A. Crary & R. Read (Eds.), *The New Wittgenstein*. London: Routledge.

Crowell, S. (2013). *Normativity and Phenomenology in Husserl and Heidegger*. Cambridge: Cambridge University Press.

Dreyfus, H. (1991). *Being-in-the-World: A Commentary on Heidegger's Being and Time, Division 1*. Cambridge, MA: MIT Press.

Egan, D., Reynolds, S., & Wendland, A. (2013). *Wittgenstein and Heidegger*. London: Routledge.

Fay, T. (1992). The Hermeneutical Phenomenology of Language in the Later Heidegger and Wittgenstein. *Dialogos*, 59, pp. 19–35.

Gier, N. F. (1981). *Wittgenstein and Phenomenology: A Comparative Study of the Later Wittgenstein, Husserl, Heidegger, and Merleau-Ponty*. New York: State University of New York Press.

Gier, N. F. (1990). Wittgenstein's Phenomenology Revisited. *Philosophy Today*, 34(3), pp. 273–288.

Glendinning, S. (1998). *On Being with Others: Heidegger, Derrida, Wittgenstein*. London: Routledge.

Hacker, P. M. S. (2003). Wittgenstein, Carnap and the New American Wittgenstei-nians. *The Philosophical Quarterly*, 53(210), pp. 1–23.

Haugeland, J. (2013). *Dasein Disclosed: John Haugeland's Heidegger*. Cambridge, MA: Harvard University Press.

Heidegger, H. (1977). The Question Concerning Technology. In W. Lovitt (Ed.), *The Question Concerning Technology and Other Essays*. New York: Harper & Row.

Heidegger, M. (1960). *Sein und Zeit*. Tübingen: Niemeyer.

Heidegger, M. (1962). *Being and Time*. New York: Harper & Row.

Heidegger, M. (1969). *Discourse on Thinking*. New York: Harper & Row.

Hintikka, J., & Hintikka, M. (1986). *Investigating Wittgenstein*. Oxford: Blackwell.

O'Rourke, J. (2018). *Expression and Silence: The Language of Phenomenology in Wittgenstein and Heidegger*. PhD Thesis. Retrieved from https://aran.library.nuigalway.ie/handle/10379/15156

Okrent, M. (1988). *Heidegger's Pragmatisme: Understanding, Being and the Critique of Metaphysics*. New York: Cornell University Press.

Okrent, M. (2013). Heidegger's Pragmatism Redux. In A. Malachowski (Ed.), *The Cambridge Companion to Pragmatism*. Cambridge: Cambridge University Press.

Park, B.-C. (1998). *Phenomenological Aspects of Wittgenstein's Philosophy*. Dordrecht, Boston, and London: Kluwer.

Reeder, H. P. (1989). Wittgenstein Never Was a Phenomenologist. *JBSP. Journal of the British Society for Phenomenology*, 20, pp. 49–68.

Richter, D. (2007). Did Wittgenstein Disagree with Heidegger? *Review of Contemporary Philosophy*, 6. Retrieved from www.academia.edu/2523162/Did_Wittgenstein_Disagree_with_Heidegger

Rorty, R. (1991). *Essays on Heidegger and Others, in Philosophical Papers 2*. Cambridge: Cambridge University Press.

Stone, A. S. (2006). Heidegger and Carnap on the Overcoming of Metaphysics. In S. Mulhall (Ed.), *Heidegger* (pp. 217–244). Aldershot: Ashgate.

Taylor, C. (1985). *Philosophical Papers 1 and 2*. Cambridge: Cambridge University Press.

Von Wright, G. H. (1982). Wittgenstein in Relation to His Times. In B. McGuinness (Ed.), *Wittgenstein and His Time*. Oxford: Basil Blackwell.

Von Wright, G. H. (1993). *The Tree of Knowledge and Other Essays*. New York: Koln, E.J. Brill.

Wittgenstein, L. (1953). *Philosophische Untersuchungen* (Translated as *Philosophical Investigations* [in German and English], Rev. 4th ed., by G. E. M. Anscombe, P. M. S. Hacker, & J. Schulte). Chichester, West Sussex, UK and Malden, MA: Wiley-Blackwell, 2009.

Wittgenstein, L. (1967). *Zettel*. Oxford: Blackwell.

Wittgenstein, L. (1977). *Remarks on Color*. Berkeley: University of California Press.

Wittgenstein, L. (1998). *Den ukjente dagboken*. Oslo: Spartacus forlag.

Wittgenstein, L. (2001). *Philosophical Investigations*. Oxford: Blackwell Publishers.

Wittgenstein, L. (2005). *Tractacus Logico Philosophicus*. London: Routledge.

Wittgenstein, L., & Waismann, F. (2003). *The Voices of Wittgenstein: The Vienna Circle* (G. P. Baker, Ed.; G. P. Baker, M. Mackert, J. Connolly, & V. Politis, Trans.). New York: Routledge.

Part 2

Nothingness in educational practice

6 Towards a theory of nothing in education

You might think, why try to cover both Heidegger and Wittgenstein in the quest for a theory of nothing? They certainly have their place in very different philosophical corners and to link such philosophers, who themselves have a difficult style, may restrict the quest for nothing. The distinctions between these two thinkers, often claimed to have been the two most influential philosophers of the 20th century, are indeed more readily apparent than what unites them. This is in line with Richter (2007, p. 1) who finds it interesting "*how two thinkers could be thought to be both so different and so alike*". Moreover, Richter (2007, p. 11) notes that

> it is true that Wittgenstein does characterize Heidegger's use of language as like a wheel in the language machine, he does not state categorically that it is an idle wheel. He considers the possibility that it might engage (eingreift) with other wheels, and does not rule out this possibility.

In the following, I will show how their terminology and terms may resonate like two calibrated wheels on the same wagon on the way to nothing (a theory of nothing). This is an attempt a concurrent critical reading of Wittgenstein and Heidegger despite the fact that neither ever obviously writes in relational way in terms of the other. The concurrent reading takes shape in what Wittgenstein might call a conceptual *family resemblance*, wherein some latent hermeneutical possibilities underlying the obvious differences come into view. In this chapter, the purpose is to embrace this possibility along with its potential pitfalls and advantages and hence engage different language(-games) and styles of thinking and writing. Therefore, it might be too ambitious to interrelate aspects of Heidegger and Wittgenstein's philosophies in order to enlist both of them on a quest for "a theory of nothing". Nevertheless, I think it is worth a try. In the following, I will show how their terminology and terms may resonate towards a theory of nothing. I will

DOI: 10.4324/9781003222231-8

concentrate on being-in-the-world and language games, technology and equipment, Gelassenheit and letting-go, projection and "grammar", thereby showing that Nothing itself is made possible.

Being-in-the-world and the language game

For Heidegger (1962), being-in-the-world and human existence are fundamentally temporal in the sense that they are always (or at least, most of the time) caught up in networks of past, present and future events, some of which are taken to be more fundamental to our well-being than others. We inscribe certain options and courses of events with values and qualities essential to our feeling of self, to our identity and to our belonging in the world. Hence, the world possesses certain meaning-structures through which we may improve our being-in-the-world. Moreover, the term being is central in being-in-the world, or to be more precise being-there. Being "there"[1] has a special meaning because "Dasein" means to relate to a type of existence/being by anticipating one's own existence in the uniqueness of the moment. Being present in the "here and now" in unique isolation, "there" can, therefore, challenge existence and jeopardise existence. Existence or Dasein can put oneself at risk, conceal and open oneself.

In parallel to being-in-the-world and in the socially conditioned meaning, the term "language-game" is meant to place emphasis on the fact that speaking language is part of an activity, or of a life-form[2] (Wittgenstein, 1953). Wittgenstein's (1953) idea is that the meaning of its word is its use in a *language game*. A language game is a set of practices and rules whereby we perform actions and use words. For example, chess has a language game, because there are special words for the pieces, and the word "check" means something special in chess because of a special possible ways of following rules, that is Shannon (1950, p. 49) states that

> In a typical chess position there will be about 32 possible moves with 32 possible replies-already this creates 1,024 possibilities. Most chess games last 40 moves or more for each side. So the total number of possible variations in an average game is about $1012°$.

This is very different from the language game of hockey, where "check" is not a board position but the act of slamming into someone in a particular way. One of Wittgenstein's (1953) decisive insights is that the rules regulating language use cannot be placed in any position outside the language itself, because they must necessarily be formulated through the language they are meant to regulate. One rule can be articulated in endless ways, and each articulation is nothing more than precisely a formulation. One explanation of a rule is not to present it as an essence like that which is conveyed and internalised in a cognitive rule database. Comprehension of a rule lies in learning to participate in the activity and to follow the rule in new situations, to be able to ask about details concerning the rule and eventually to be able to offer a formulation of it. Being able to apprehend an explanation of a rule demands an entire set of prerequisites (cf. form of life, see endnote). It demands an intimate knowledge of the language of which it is a part. In summary, to understand a language entails being within the language already, like a type of being-in-the-world (Heidegger, 1962) or language game (Wittgenstein, 1953).

This is apparent in the way that the teacher urges students to inquire and dwell in the "personal" or "individual" aspects of situations. For example, in thinking about education, different dominant notions often arise. This could be pursued in the manner of Wittgenstein (in his work on conceptual analysis with the example of "games"); it would be possible to ask about the use of the word knowledge, learning, student, competence, teaching, reflection, supervision, success, failure, trust, in different contexts and by different educational people. In response to this predicament, I might ask a Heideggerian question: What is the foundation of a situation where the (interwoven) concept of education, learning and competence is an issue? So, the crucial question is: When in the present course, does study (cf. Chapter 7) mean to contemplate, ponder or ruminate within the full situation as a worlded being? Furthermore, it is perhaps unhelpful for teachers or students to bring into discussions dichotomies such as university and home, work and leisure, public and private, because being-in-the-world could be less genuine. The slaying of dichotomies is an issue. The relevance of this in the teaching of higher education is that it opens doors to the student's engagement with course content in a very full manner. No longer is the course a confined aspect in the student's life. Teaching and education are not abstract, unrelated to the student, scientific, objective or purely intellectual. It is like education itself – something that takes over oneself. Accordingly, an important realisation for students is that there is no separation between their personal situation and their education, work or university life.

Technology and equipment

Maybe Wittgenstein (1953, 1969) ponders the same question as René Descartes: How to find a solid ground for reasoning? Descartes' (2016) answer – I think, therefore I am – was to postulate two separated ontological substances: pure cognition (res cogitans) and physical bodies with spatial extension (res extensa). Wittgenstein's (1953) solution can be translated into the slogan: we perform, therefore we are. So, Wittgenstein's (1953) answer differs because, firstly, there's not an abstract "I" but a shared social language with rules, techniques and performance. In on certainty, Wittgenstein (1969, §341) writes: "*That is to say, the question that we raise and our doubts depend on the fact that some propositions are exempt from doubt, are as it were like hinges on which those turn*". The metaphor Wittgenstein (1969) uses "*are as it were like hinges on which those turn*" is interesting. "*If I want the door to turn, the hinges must stay put*" (Wittgenstein, 1969, §343). We can interpret the example of these hinges as denoting something about the use of technology: for Wittgenstein, the use of equipment (such as language) is not an isolated inner cognition but a finite bodily practice, which can succeed or fail in concrete, socially shared situations. These performances and techniques are thus revealed as a solid ground of reasoning and could be said to be techno-like, as something that is presupposed when we think and that we trust, without having explicit knowledge of it. Even though Wittgenstein never used the term technology (as far as I know), it seems reasonable to say that what we take for granted (often with no explicit knowledge as a form of aspect blindness) rests on form of life and language games.

Heidegger (1962), however, also considers our trust in technology and *equipmentality*. Equipmentality relates to a phrase of Heidegger's (1962): "readiness-to-hand". Something that is ready-to-hand has a status as a tool, in some sense an extension of our body. The lighter sitting on my desk beside this computer is ready-to-hand because I can use it at any time for a pre-defined activity (lighting a cigarette). What makes the modern technology differ from use of tools in the past is the manner in which they are used. The term technology derives from the Greek word *techné*, used in the sense of allowing man to bring forth the hidden essence of a substance that was being affected by a tool. Today it is the river that is built into the modern hydraulic power plant and set upon so that it can provide water pressure. Moreover, Heidegger (1977, p. 17, 26) clearly states that:

> "*Everywhere everything is ordered to stand by, to be immediately at hand, indeed, to stand there just so that it may be on call for a further ordering. Whatever is ordered about in this way has its own standing. We call it the standing-reserve [Bestand]*". . . . *Thus* . . . "*Where Enframing holds sway, the regulating and securing of standing in reserve marks all. They no longer even allow their own fundamental characteristic of revealing to appear. . . . Thus the challenging Enframing conceals not only a former way of revealing or bringing-forth, but it conceals itself and with it that wherein unconcealment, e.g., truth, comes to pass.*"

Modern educational technology (cf. Chapter 3) also lets the new quality of being come into presence, but it does so by way of challenging being, rushing it, urging, demanding that it brings immediate economic income. A part of nature is disregarded and forgotten in its integrity and becomes meaningful only as a resource.

In summary, the place where these two philosophers come together is not just in phenomenology, but also that both see language and the "Being of human beings" (Heidegger) or the "Form of life" (Wittgenstein) as being, in a deep sense, defined by the technology and tools employed by human beings.

How can such insights be translated into education? Indeed, a persistent problem in higher education and teaching is that we want to turn our students into radical, if short-term, cartesian figures. For example, students will often treat the notion of vagueness in such a way that all concepts without sharp boundaries are considered vague. What about terms such as (indeterminate) learning, (embodied) knowledge and (solid) competence? If we suppose that these notions can be used in this vague and uncertain way, then the upshot is often that the student dismisses as invalid all terms, theories and perspectives employing concepts and phenomena that admit borderline cases. What can be ordered and what cannot be ordered in terms of learning (outcome), (valid) knowledge and (clear-cut) competence? Perhaps the answer to this is that the student must learn to dwell and analyse thoughts and arguments in a way that is sensitive to the contexts, language games and being-in-the-world (i.e. the blind spots as "hinges" and ready-to-hand technology can be worth revealing) in which they occur. A term or phenomenon in an illustration, theory, argument, etc. may be vague, but the reasoning and argument may not trade upon this vagueness. Or the vagueness may weaken the argument, though not in a serious way given its general intents and purposes. Finally, a phenomenon may contain crucial terms that are *hopelessly* vague; a common and interesting expression indicating that we really do not understand the range of application of such terms (perhaps Nothing is a good example). This may sound like a platitude. I don't think that I have ever heard anyone come right out and say: "Ignore context; it doesn't matter". But turning to context represents an important departure from the standard way of looking at equipmentality, ready-made and applied to ordering outcomes and educational technology (cf. Chapter 3).

Gelassenheit (releasement) and letting-go

We may be held captive, "frozen" positive or very frustrated by a dominant technological way of being. Heidegger (1977) sketches an alternative to the predominant technological way of being. Because technology (*Gestell*) *is* primarily an attitude towards those properties of the world that allow for their exploitation, it seems clear that we are always to some extent determined by a technological relationship with the world. This is not to say, of course, that the world does not contain other, different aspects, different possibilities of relating to it and consequently to our self-understanding. One alternative is the attitude of *Gelassenheit*, in which we are freed from the technological imperative through releasing the things in the world:

> *we can act otherwise. We can use technical devices, and yet with proper use also keep ourselves so free of them, that we may let go of them any time . . . But will not saying both yes and no this way to technical devices make our relation to technology ambivalent and insecure? On the contrary! Our relation to technology will become wonderfully simple and relaxed . . . I would call this comportment toward technology which expresses 'yes' and at the same time 'no', by an old word, releasement towards things [Gelassenheit].*
>
> (Heidegger, 1977, pp. 53–54)

That is to say, technology cannot be denied or abolished, because it is too much a part of our being-in-the-world. As such, it exists neither "out there", as a physical fact, nor "in there" as cognitive representations; it is part of our embodied being, of our way of relating to the world. For example, the educational apparatus (i.e. detailed learning outcome schemes) are no more cases and kinds of enframing than are the man at the switchboard and the engineer in the drafting room. Each of these in its own way belongs as an available resource (to be ordered, just order!). However, technology is never the essence of technology in the sense of a genus. There is always the possibility of revealing that is a "destining", namely *the way that challenges forth* (Heidegger, 1977, p. 335). In a somewhat similar vein, Wittgenstein addresses the possibility and necessity of releasement or letting go.

Letting-go

Letting-go rests on the assumptions that we do not often see the sheer variety and richness present in our languages; that language is not one homogeneous whole. Rather, it is comprised of an indeterminate number of language games that reach every aspect of our lives (Wittgenstein, 1953). These language games are based upon our different human activities, which constitute our experiences and our existence. As such, experiences come into and go out of existence corresponding to the changes in shared human activities. Therefore, it is reasonable to state that letting go of possible experiences and activities is a complex issue, or to borrow a better formulation:

> *Letting go is, in some way, a theory of potential. It shows us the many avenues our life could take us, the tangled webs of the world, the endless possibilities. And also the limits of our potential, the fact that we can never do everything we could do. In a world of potentials, letting go unmasks our capacity for it.*

(Rehn & Taalas, 2009, p. 94)

However, "*umasking our capacity for it*" is easier said than done. One consequence of this complex web is that the educational "failure" could be the result of any number and combination of language games, thus complicating any attempt to untangle them. It also means, as Wittgenstein (1953) contends, that no one approach could be used to successfully treat most all cases. More specifically, every approach would have to be individualised to address the specific ailment from which the student (and certainly also teachers and researchers) suffers. Wittgenstein (1953) utilises an indirect method of discourse to guide us on our journey towards "getting a handle" on the problem. "*The same or almost the same points*," Wittgenstein (1953, Preface) writes, "*were always being approached afresh from different directions, and new sketches made*". This criss-crossing all through language and thought affords one the opportunity to encounter a problem from multiple perspectives and the possibility of getting of unburdening ourselves of them. Wittgenstein (1953, §144) elaborates on this indirect method:

> *But was I trying to draw someone's attention to the fact that he is capable of imaging that? – I wanted to put that picture before him, and his acceptance of the picture consists in his now being inclined to regard a given case differently: that is, to compare it with this rather than that set of pictures. I have only changed his way of looking at things.*

As mentioned, this change of perspective is not an easily accomplished feat; the educational tendency of "craving for generality" exerts a powerful influence over us. Maybe constant movement helps us notice what may be that hardest to see, namely, what is directly before our eyes. Wittgenstein (1953) contends that we take for granted our primary assumptions upon which we build our world view, effectively blinding us to the ramifications of our misrelationship. This is how the (indirect) investigation must proceed, because we have a tendency to settle for one perspective. In the next section, "projection and grammar", it is possible to see how "*looking at things*" differently may work.

Projection and grammar

It is important to keep in mind that *Understanding* is an existential aspect; it is involved in the nature of *possibility* and it has the nature of *projection*.
  Heidegger (1996, p. 136) asks the question:

> *"Why does understanding always penetrate into possibilities according to all the essential dimension of what can be disclosed to it?"* His direct answer is that *"It is because the understanding has in itself the existential structure which we call 'projection.'"*

Projection thus means a sort of *antecedent comprehending*. This "projective" understanding (*Sicht*) has access to both beings and Being (Dasein), that is to say, it moves in two ways:

1   Towards the *world*, that is significance (as the totality of involvements) that is the understanding of (Zuhanden) entities or applicable objects within the world; this understanding may be compared to how students manipulate analytical tools, that is writing text, applying curriculum terms without having any problem with doing so.
2   Towards the *for-the-sake-of-which*, that is Dasein (being-there) gaining access to itself self-understanding. This may point towards how students at first might understand themselves and their education and (future) jobs differently.

In other words, the *projecting* of the *understanding* has the *possibility* of developing itself; that is, the understanding has the possibility of referring back to itself, of "understanding itself". As such, being-there understands itself in terms of possibilities. Furthermore, the character of understanding as projection is such that the understanding does not grasp thematically that upon which it projects, that is to say, possibilities. Grasping it in such a manner would take away from what is projected its very character as a possibility and would reduce it to the given contents which we have in mind, whereas projection throws before itself the possibility as possibility and lets it *be* as such. As projecting, understanding is the kind of Being of being-there in which it is its possibilities as possibilities.

Grammar

Wittgenstein makes a suggestion that may have some bearing on Heidegger's prioritisation of futurity and projection, if only to give another example of use. Wittgenstein (2002, p. 109) writes:

We could, of course, imagine a realm of the unborn, future events, whence they come into reality and pass into the realm of the past; and, if we think in terms of this metaphor, we may be surprised that the future should appear less existent than the past.

The major source of grammatical prejudices, illusions and the notion that the "*future should appear less existent*" is the inclination, when we are involved in educational activities, to impose features of the methods we use to represent phenomena on the phenomena itself. For example, we may take the sky itself to be red – but simply because we are looking at it through red-tinted glasses. Or perhaps we take the spatial world itself to be constituted of inches, feet and yards – because these are the units in the system with which we measure the world. "*We predicate of the thing what lies in the method of representing it*" (Wittgenstein, 1953, §104). What if predetermined curriculum endpoint and learning outcome (cf. Chapter 3) as (techno) *methods* in a dominant way (and illusionary) desperately wants to predict the essential student understanding required in higher educa-tion? Grammar may be the remedy and the point where experience and the world, so to speak, touch – it is an indeterminate place (Wittgenstein, 1953). When speaking of truth, we often appeal to what is the case, that is to the immutable truth of reality. The truth of a student action and per-formance is very often justified by comparison with the actual matter (i.e. learning outcome and curriculum endpoint). What Wittgenstein (1953) sought, upon successfully avoiding the perils of matter-of-factness, was the stretching that forced one to look at matters one had never considered before. Perhaps what had intellectual value above all else for Wittgenstein (1953) was the spontaneous idea which come in a flash obliterating in an instant confusion and incoherence. It is tempting to ask what kind of value the spontaneous idea inherits in higher education?

Educational practitioners (i.e. students, teachers, researchers) are thus initiated into a practice by learning to enact relevant distinctions in prac-tice, with each new experience enlarging one's "grammatical" (Wittgen-stein, 1953) sense of what their proper usage is, namely, the sense of what in the future can possibly follow on from one's experiences hitherto. We thus come to experience certain situations initially as difficulties, to the extent that, trained student of an educational practice, have already come to embody certain expectations, anticipations and projections as a conse-quence of our learning certain ways of doing things (i.e. vignettes 1–7 in Chapter 7). It is when the flow of our work is disrupted and we become disoriented, not knowing how next to "go on" (Wittgenstein, 1953, §154), that we feel we face a difficulty, which may be engulfed with projections (from Nothing).

Narrowing the scope

These are (nothing) experiences and performances that often precede our theoretical knowledge and lie behind a technological world that is always ready for use. The theory of nothing is about pre-epistemological and often pre-language elements that challenge our existence, (self-)understanding and way of being.

As a point of departure, it is possible to outline six aspects that can be included in a theory of Nothing.

- Indeterminateness – the term horizon may describe the indeterminate nature and always already potential of nothing, which includes some form of passive compulsion; hence, expressions like 'We do not decide our experiences ourselves!? Experiences force themselves on us!' This enforced indeterminateness is further illustrated in a radical way in the statement: *Höher als die Wirklichkeit steht die Möglichkeit* (higher than reality stands possibility) (Heidegger, 1962, p. 38).
- Personal – this aspect makes it possible to see the connection between nothingness and personal experience. Experience (*erfahrung*) as an unpredictable journey and a hazardous life project may inherit the openness of nothing. The most important thing is that Heidegger (1962) did not seek an understanding or mere knowledge, but a special kind of inner experience, which is the feeling of existence as the coming-to-be of newness.
- Embodiment – embodied sense of sight.
- Skills-based – skills such as the utilisation of tools (hence, the centrality of tools and equipmentality).
- Intimacy-based – this aspect could shed light on the relationship between language game and not-being-at-home (nothing).
- Can break free of the language – here, the crucial point is how the "inexpressible" can be expressible and vice versa.[3]

In light of these six points (and perhaps especially illuminated by the last point), when one is asked to give an explanation of a theory of Nothing, it is tempting to reply that we can adduce only exterior facts about Nothing. One can describe facts about human instincts, the natural history of man, educational practice, etc., but in principle, it is impossible to fully describe "the opening of the Open". The point, in both Wittgenstein and Heidegger, is that any explanation they would give is necessarily given from *within* the Open and, therefore, cannot go outside the Open to describe its genesis. Even though it is a controversial statement (perhaps especially with regard to Wittgenstein's early philosophy), both Heidegger (1962) and Wittgenstein (1953) take it as one of their primary tasks to describe the opening of the Open (although in radically different ways).

For Heidegger (1962), chaos, primordially understood, is the self-opening abyss, the self-opening nothingness, meaning that it is the abyss that opens into the Open within which beings can be. However, Wittgenstein (1953) is not trying to resolve whatever a practice may work but is rather describing the wonder (cf. Chapter 5) and grammatical context (*language games*) in which efficacy-claims become regarded *as* certain. Not "backsliding" into explanation of things as they are in-themselves (Rorty, 1991). Wittgenstein (1953, §371) shows instead how "*Essence* is expressed by grammar". It is important to note that "essence" means the creation of new language games and linguistic practices.

Moreover, Heidegger (1962) finds in anxiety (Angst derived from nothing) the basic experiences which expose being-there to the groundlessness, abyss and finitude of its possibilities. According to Heidegger (1962), *anxiety* differs from other forms of fear and dread in that in anxiety we do not fear anything particular – other human beings, animals, natural disasters, diseases, etc. – that would threaten us. Rather, in anxiety, we experience that our entire familiar world with all its beings collapses into itself and the world has the character of (completely) lacking significance. As such, anxiety robs being-there of the possibility of understanding itself. The "uncanniness" (*Unheimlichkeit*, which literally means "unhomelike-ness") of anxiety exposes the individual being-there to the basic fact that it is "not-at-home" (*Un-zuhause*) within the familiar world of the one that it has slid into and confronts it with the task of personally facing up to choosing its own possibilities.

Anxiety is an experience of a fundamental phenomenon of the very horizon of the *there* of being-there (*Da* of Dasein), that is, of what Heidegger (1962) called the "nothing and nowhere" of the beings. Heidegger (2000) explicitly tells us that anxiety is the experience of Nothing as Being with the character of *phenomenon*. Consequently, this "nothing" does not constitute something like the "not" of a being. Anxiety is a possibility of being-there. It pounces on being-there unexpectedly and involuntarily; it overwhelms and conquers it. With regard to being-there's relation to Nothing, being-there does not exactly find itself in an experience that makes or even lets Nothing appear. Nothing finds being-there and discloses itself to it. In this meeting, Nothing escapes the measures of being-there, and being-there is "at the mercy" of Nothing, without being able to fully know whence Nothing came upon it. In the existential mode of experiencing anxiety, Nothing simply "drags" being-there in its *there*.

Notes

1 In his work *Being and Time*, Heidegger (1962) takes as his point of departure that being-there (Dasein) is the only form of existence/being that can provide an answer as to the meaning of being, and being-there (Dasein), therefore, has a special status. What is it that is so special about being-there and why is it distinguished from other entities? Heidegger (1962, §4) responds:

> *Dasein is a being that occurs not only among beings. Dasein is ontically distinguished by the fact that, in its very Being, that Being is an issue for it. . . . This being is distinguished by the fact that it is opened for this being by virtue of and through its being. . . . Dasein's ontic distinction lies in the fact that it is ontological.*

2 The notion of "form of life" appears only a few times in Wittgenstein's published writings. However, despite the unclear meaning of the notion, Wittgenstein scholars have agreed from the outset that this is the most significant concept in his philosophy (Gier, 1990), and, at the same time *opaque,* even *impenetrable* (Kishik, 2008), since the author did not use it in a technical way and did not provide any definition of it. At the same time, this notion enabled a dialogue between Wittgenstein and a broader philosophical, anthropological and political tradition.

3 Wittgenstein (2005) may be understood to claim that the ethical falls out of the domain of the factual, hence leaving no conclusion from being to duty. That is to say, there is no "translation" between the expressible and the inexpressible of the ethical or aesthetics but only a "leap" – just as Heidegger (1978) said in *Identity and Difference* that the sentence makes a "sentence" (Sprung) in the sense of a "leap", and we only leap into an abyss, where we potentially leap and release ourselves (Heidegger, 1978).

References

Descartes, R. (2016). *Discourse on Method and Meditations on First Philosophy.* London: Createspace Independent Publishing Platform.

Gier, N. F. (1990). Wittgenstein's Phenomenology Revisited. *Philosophy Today*, 34(3), pp. 273–288.

Heidegger, H. (1977). The Question Concerning Technology. In W. Lovitt (ed.), *The Question Concerning Technology and Other Essays.* New York: Harper & Row.

Heidegger, M. (1962). *Being and Time.* New York: Harper & Row.

Heidegger, M. (1978). *Identität und Differenz.* Neske: Pfullingen.

Heidegger, M. (1996). *Being and Time: A Translation of Sein und Zeit.* Albany, NY: State University of New York Press.

Heidegger, M. (2000). *Introduction to Metaphysics* (G. Fried & R. Polt, Trans.). London: Yale University Press.

Kishik, D. (2008). *Wittgenstein's Form of Life (To Imagine a Form of Life, I).* London and New York: Continuum.

Rehn, A., & Taalas, S. (2009). On Wittgenstein and Management at Rest: Prolegomena to a Philosophy of Problems. *Philosophy of Management*, 7(2), pp. 89–95.

Richter, D. (2007). Did Wittgenstein Disagree With Heidegger? *Review of Contemporary Philosophy*, 6, pp. 1–43.

Rorty, R. (1991). *Essays on Heidegger and Others, in Philosophical Papers 2*. Cambridge: Cambridge University Press.

Shannon, C. (1950). A Chess-Playing Machine. *Scientific American*, pp. 48–51.

Wittgenstein, L. (1953). *Philosophische Untersuchungen* (Translated as *Philosophical Investigations* [in German and English], Rev. 4th ed., by G. E. M. Anscombe, P. M. S. Hacker, & J. Schulte). Chichester, West Sussex, UK and Malden, MA: Wiley-Blackwell, 2009.

Wittgenstein, L. (1969). *On Certainty* (G. E. M. Anscombe & G. H. von Wright, Eds.; D. Paul & G. E. M. Anscombe, Trans.). Oxford: Blackwell.

Wittgenstein, L. (2002). *The Blue and the Brown Book*. Oxford: John Wiley and Sons.

Wittgenstein, L. (2005). *Tractacus Logico Philosophicus*. London: Routledge.

7 Vignettes and examples of educational technology and nothing

In this chapter, vignettes and examples from educational research are presented in order to show the potential of nothing-in-technology and the significance of technology-in-nothing when educational actors become educational. Heidegger's (1962) initial question (the question of the meaning of Being and hence Nothing) is heavily metaphysical, but it is designed so as to direct us towards the primacy of worldly affairs and hence the centrality of the conception being-in-the-world and forms of life. "World" in a Heideggerian sense is not a way of characterising those entities which Dasein (Being-there) essentially is not; it is rather characteristic of Being-there (Da-sein) itself. It possesses a pre-ontological signification. In a sense, we already know the answer to the question, and the question is given its form and content on the basis of this prior understanding. The way to approach the problem, then, is not by abstaining from worldly interests in a distanced and analytical, cartesian way, but rather to immerse the analysis in the everyday world of human activity; to "*see what shows itself in 'entities' within the world*" (Heidegger, 1962, p. 92), and I might add, what shows itself as possibilities and potentiality. In parallel, Wittgenstein (1977) also advocates a kind of a phenomenological investigation. To paraphrase Wittgenstein (1980), phenomenology only establishes the possibilities, and phenomenology aims to exhibit the possibilities (and therefore the essence) of phenomena.

As mentioned earlier in Chapter 4, some Heideggerian and Wittgenstein-inspired educational research exists, and even (phenomenological) existential and personal experience-oriented themes have been unfolded. However, to my knowledge, research focusing mainly on educational Nothing (-experiences) is non-existent. In the light of different (phenomenological) data sources, I present some illuminating examples of Nothing in educational practice, which makes it possible to trace some of the paths whereby educational participants become educational. More specifically,

DOI: 10.4324/9781003222231-9

through the use of examples and (first-hand) data from research conducted by Rennemo and Vaag (2018),[1] it is possible to show how technological experience and existential spheres and transformations among students open up interpretations of Angst or "nothing practice".

Heideggerian and Wittgenstein-inspired concepts or aspects are used as main headings; technology-being and Angst/Nothing in education are used when presenting vignettes. Under these headings, other terms are used such as equipment-technology, letting-go-"Gelassenheit", being-there/being-in-the-world-language game, projection-"grammar" (cf. Chapter 6).[2] However, this does not mean that each concept is an independent category that alone describes a phenomenon, nor does it mean that Heidegger's and Wittgenstein's concepts occur in a logical order in the phenomenon through which educational participants undergo the experience of nothing and begin to act and re-invent educational practice. It is important to note that these three aspects are phenomenological in nature; that is, they are about deep meanings and are not primarily psychological traits/attitudes or sociological manifestations (norms, roles, etc.). They are something more and beyond that; they are based on a being-in-the-world, language game and existence that rests on a reflective structure. The deep meanings may show how educational participants understand themselves in a world representing ontological rather than ontic aspects of educational practice.

At the end of this section, a new categorisation of nothing is presented based on the data; that is to say, terms such as being-reserved, being-slow, being-blank, being-ecstatic (projection) may show important aspects of an indeterminate Nothing phenomenon.

I begin with an analysis of the perceived dominant condition of education conceptualised as Technology-being. Technology describes how education participants relate to ready-to-hand, tool-based and a sort of automatised practice, which in turn are relevant in the way they constitute their genuine understanding of the horizon of possibilities within technology. For this purpose, I think that Heidegger's concept of technology and Wittgenstein's equipmentality are a relevant entrance for readers to become familiar with one of the modern conditions of educational life as it is perceived by researchers and educational participants (in my case, by students in higher education). Educational participants, as human beings, are born and thrown into a complex world where they have to learn to master skills and tools simply to be able to cope in the world. Technology thus influences educational actors' understanding of possibilities, as well as their experiences and life projects. It is in technology that educational beings are introduced to tools and where tools become handy and technologised.

Technological-being in education

These vignettes are based on reflection notes from students in a knowledge management programme at master grade level. The data were collected between 2008 and 2013 and consist of notes from three classes (approximately 105 students). The students are asked to reflect on experiences after their final master thesis. These are experiences concerning partner collaboration (students can be up to three persons doing the master thesis), research challenges (i.e. how to go on with theory, method, data collection, data analysis, the writing process), personal development, etc. Tracing such experiences, the following is an utterance with regard to how basic hidden assumptions and prejudices are brought to light when two students-as-researchers face a discovery task in the beginning of the research process:

(1) We expected a higher degree of engagement and ownership in the developmental programme within the organisation. After all, this was adopted formally in the municipal executive board and through the description of the challenge in municipal plans and other documents. Nevertheless, it should not come as a surprise that we experienced a lack of action and ownership despite the adoption of the overall decisions and plans. These are precisely the "deficiencies" that traditional objectivist and structural approaches have been criticised for! As we mentioned during the discussion concerning the research issue, it may, therefore, be relevant to ask ourselves whether we might be under the influence of an inordinately structural and mechanistic view of knowledge in our approach to research work. We have been caught in a kind of "positivism trap"? We were challenged on the view of knowledge that we asserted was the basis for our approach (practice-based), and we were confronted with our own previous attitudes, now disapproved, when we eventually perceived that our anticipations were too largely associated with a structural view of knowledge. We had to acknowledge that Wheatley (1992, in Irgens, 2011, p. 196) is correct to a certain extent in maintaining that *"we are prisoners of a mechanistic world view"*.

The statement that it is *"relevant to ask ourselves whether we might be under the influence of an inordinately structural and mechanistic view of knowledge in our approach to research"* suggests that it is difficult to free ourselves from the forced notion of there always being a problem "at hand",

and that it is a challenge to learn to wait on beings to reveal their ontological depth, potential and possibilities, or in Wittgenstein (2005) terms freeing us from images, illusions and misleading analogies that hold us captive. Clearly, there is a potential for improvement regarding an attentive listening to being's (members of the county council) approaching it carefully, with respect, with no egoistic attempt at dominating it cognitively. The students' general structure of being-in-the-world is at the same time characteristic of specific properties of the world and a specific attitude of towards the world (i.e. structural view of knowledge) in the beginning of the research process. It is this particular attitude towards those properties of the research object that allow said "object" to become a resource for exploitation. Technology is the unconditional establishment (Heidegger, 1977) or *"mechanistic world view"*, posed by students' self-assertion that prevails against the pure draft, by which the unheard of centre for the moment draws all pure forces to itself. The next vignette pays attention to rased/technological habits and type of self-understanding that can potentially be challenged.

---

(2) Through our work on the master's thesis, we have undergone a learning process that can be described as single-circuit learning. Through our experiences in the project, we have learnt that we can adapt the structures in the breakthrough method so that they fit our daily life to a greater extent. We discuss whether teachers in the group have undergone some form of double-circuit learning, but have we ourselves experienced this in conjunction with the master's thesis? We have not changed our basic assumptions regarding students and learning through our work. The work involving students with learning challenges and weak motivation has instead reinforced the basic assumptions we had at the outset. As a point of departure, teaching must take the students at the point where they are.

Students who collaborated on the master's thesis characterise the work as *"single-circuit learning"*, *"where we have"* . . . *not* . . . *"changed our basic assumptions regarding students and learning"*. In other words, they have applied the tools that are already rased and established in a daily practice, or to paraphrase Heidegger (1977), who states that *Technology cannot simply be rejected; it is too much part of our being-in-the-world. As such, it does not simply exist "out there", but it is part of our bodily being*, of our whole way of relating to the world. Based on the claim that they "have instead reinforced the basic assumptions we had at the outset", this can be understood as a means of letting-go (of double loop learning) practice in order to keep things mindfully on track. A letting-go practice where the potential of new learning is recognised but not pursued in depth, because as a Wittgensteinian way of speaking might put it, the importance is *"the restful potential and letting go unmasks our capacity for it."* (Rehn & Taalas, 2009, p. 94). The importance of keeping things mindfully on track is also discussed in the next vignette:

---

(3) For us, the master's degree study in knowledge and innovation leadership has been an informative and useful process. As rectors, we are committed to ensuring that our schools are learning organisations in practice. It is largely a question of good leadership at the individual school and governmental department level.

When working in parallel with our jobs as rectors, the study programme and writing of the master's thesis have presented us with many challenges, in a positive sense. We have become more aware of our role as school leaders by developing ourselves as thoughtful practitioners. By replenishing our minds with new knowledge, we have enhanced our ability to remain focused on processes in conjunction with school administration, organising teaching, choice of work methods, learning outcomes for the students and the overall learning results. Through our research, we have learnt that there are several pathways to achieving good solutions.

Competence-based education is predominant, particularly with regard to the notion that processes seem to be important in terms of *"school governance, organising teaching, choice of work methods, learning outcomes for the students and overall learning results"* (cf. Chapter 3).

In a technological tendency, educationalists (i.e. educational practitioners, in this vignette two students who work as principals) use technology to increase the likelihood of achieving essentially non-(nothing) educational and non-educational means such as increasing test scores and learning outcomes (such a tendency is confirmed by research, i.e. Johnson & Johnson, 1991). Moreover, "non-nothing educational means" may be defined as preset curricular endpoints, at which not only the pupils but also themselves as students have to arrive with *"replenished knowledge"*.

In the next vignette, the student accounts for the way his personal (technological) baggage contributes to challenges and a more acknowledgeable stance in the research process:

(4) Challenges have emerged on several levels. Knowledge of what was the core production and disciplinary field of X, learning the organisation and how it is organised, and the experience of a great discrepancy in focus and understanding of the context in a topic such as management by objectives and consequence evaluation are some of these aspects. Perhaps the greatest challenge has been the discrepancy in the latter aspect. Why do I think so? I consider myself a practitioner. By that, I mean that whether they be theories, laws and regulations, standards, technical descriptions, courses or developmental work, these must all have a practical value. I have to be able to associate it with a meaning or with an understanding that can produce a result. The corporate-economic perspective is one tradition that I carry with me from my field of practice. In this tradition, most of the activities and measures taken are managed by objectives, and management by objectives is in turn associated with an economic result. This means that most of the activities I conduct are expected to produce an economic result in one way or another.

The sense of self-understanding, of being there, relies on seeing oneself "*as a practitioner*", meaning that "*whether they be theories, laws and regulations, standards, technical descriptions, courses or developmental work, these must all have a practical value.*"

Such technological accounts (e.g. theories and laws) attempt to explain human phenomena in terms of basic human interests and needs that people's actions *must* satisfy if they are all to fit together into a systematic whole (i.e. "the corporate economic perspective"). This basic student interest may be that "*this must have a practical value*". Meaning and understanding, therefore, must be created in light of, or grow out of, technology; that is to say, the "*laws, regulations, standards, technical descriptions*" that stand ready to be used (Heidegger, 1977). In a certain sense, this may be affiliated with the Wittgensteinian (1953, §431) insight that

> there is a gulf between an order and its execution. It has to be filled by the act of understanding. Only in the act of understanding is it meant that we are to do THIS. The order – why, that is nothing but sounds.

It is plausible that there will never be an interpretation that completely bridges the gulf between an order and its execution (somebody will obviously argue for a super standard connection between words and action). That is to say, we do not know, in a fully explicit sense, what Being-there we are looking for, yet we may look for it because we have clues (i.e. "*a practical value*"). Hence, there may be an ineffable dimension in understanding that has the potential of nothing-experiences and not knowing how to go on (Wittgenstein (1969). However, in the next vignette, students express their technological optimism thus:

---

(5) Not least, we have gained insight into scientific ways of working that encompass choices of methods based on the research issue, the use of sources and source referencing, not to mention training in how to express ourselves in precise terms. We have related to a large body of literature, both literature that has been a part of the syllabus in the MKIL study programme and also other specialist literature – mostly pedagogical literature. It has been challenging to select what we deem to be most relevant. We have used the Internet to a large degree to search for relevant articles and other pertinent literature, and this has also been educationally beneficial. It has been especially useful for one of us to hone skills in this area.

The students speak in light of almost three years long training in how to go and acquire skills in, for example, methodology and academic writing in order to get "*insight into scientific work methods . . . use of sources and referencing sources.*" Moreover, the measurability and utility are described and elaborated in the "total learning outcome scheme". In the master's degree programme of knowledge management, this is discussed as follows.

---

(6) Description of learning outcomes

After completing the study programme, a candidate will have the following total learning outcomes defined in terms of knowledge, skills and general competence:

Knowledge

The candidate:

- has advanced knowledge about organisation and leadership and special insight into management of knowledge work and knowledge processes in organisations.

- has detailed knowledge about recent research, scientific theories and methods that are relevant to management of knowledge work and knowledge processes in organisations.
- is able to **apply** knowledge in new areas that are relevant for management of knowledge work and knowledge processes in organisations.
- is able to **analyse** academic issues related to management of knowledge work and knowledge processes based on the discipline's history, traditions, distinctive nature and place in society.

Skills

The candidate:

- is able to **analyse** and relate critically to various sources of information and apply these for structuring and formulating academic rationales pertaining to knowledge, knowledge work and knowledge management.
- is able to analyse relevant theories, methods and interpretations and transfer them to practical and theoretical problem-solving in the management of knowledge work and knowledge processes in organisations.
- is able independently to **utilise** methods for research and academic development work that is relevant for research on management of knowledge work and knowledge processes.
- is able, under supervision, to implement an independent, delimited research and/or developmental project in line with accepted scientific methods and applicable ethical research norms.

General competence

The candidate:

- is able to **analyse** relevant academic and ethical research issues associated with management of knowledge work and knowledge processes.
- is able to **apply** his/her knowledge and skills in new areas to manage knowledge work and knowledge processes.
- is able to **convey** comprehensive, independent work and masters the terminology of the discipline.

- is able to **communicate** academic issues, analyses and conclusions within the field of knowledge management with both specialists and laymen.
- is able, through application of knowledge and skills, to perform as a reflecting practitioner in the management of knowledge work and knowledge processes.
- is able, through management of knowledge work and knowledge processes, to contribute towards creation and innovation in organisations.

The course descriptions in the curriculum contain expected learning outcomes for the individual courses in the study programme (www.nord.no/no/student/studieplaner/2021v/sider/90mkl.aspx#&acd=L%c3%a6 ringsutbytte-header). The highlighted words are my own.

The terms "*apply, analyse, use, convey, communicate*" marked in bold script in this vignette denote or embody general skills, that is a body of rational tendencies and generalised habits that in turn subordinate the vague, indeterminate and ever-not-quite experiences to clean-cut and dried measurable pieces of equipment/ends. This "learning outcome" way of being and technology (although hermeneutic in principle and always already open for possibilities) is its ability to close off other non-applicable and potentially effective forms of understanding, education and pedagogies, of the notion is not negated that there are potentially other forms of disclosure, but they are certainly muted and, therefore, not applicable and not in use. Maybe this is due to the sharp focus on beings who should present themselves only in terms of their utility, effectiveness and measurability.

It is enlightening to interpret these schematic learning outcome descriptions as indicators saying something about use of technology. For Wittgenstein (1969), the use of an artefact (i.e. schemes of learning outcome) is not an isolated inner cognition but a finite bodily practice, which is embedded in concrete social situations. These practices, performances and techniques are thus revealed as a solid ground of reasoning, apparently, as something that is presupposed when we reason and which we accept and trust, without necessarily having explicit knowledge of it and without having certainty. We succeed or fail in such shared situations. With pragmatic modesty, Wittgenstein (1969) says: "*My life consists in my being content to accept many things*" (§344).

The description of learning outcomes (which has become mandatory and presented as a universal piece of equipment (cf. OECD, 2012)) governs assessment, evaluation and testing strategies, as a kind of tool just waiting to be used, that is judgements to be signed and distributed. Perhaps principals, teachers and universities are "caught" to look at the world as a set of resources where the emphasis is on resource utilisation (i.e. learning outcome schemes) or what, in Heideggerian terms, is technology. Technological accounts attempt to explain to students phenomena of (pre-)understanding in terms of outcomes or preset curriculum end-points that seem to satisfy and fit together into a predetermined systematic whole. Indeed, Wittgenstein (1969) expresses his technological reservations about such fixed knowledge grounds thus: "*You must bear in mind that the language-game is so to speak something unpredictable. I mean: it is not based on grounds. It is not reasonable (or unreasonable). It is there – like our life*" (§559).

For the same reason (the unpredictable or indeterminate "knowledgeable" way of student being, cf. Chapter 1), we must resist an interpretation that would have us understand *technology* only as the result of a reduction of *Nothing* and this reduction only as a loss. To be sure, something is lost: what the student may have lost is her place in the world (see next chapter). But this loss may be compensated for by a gain. Without this (temporary) loss we could make no sense of a new (self-)understanding and new horizons of existence. If we see (nothing) understanding or being-nothing as an essential part of educational practice, we must also insist that it is impossible for things to present themselves to participants in education as the things they are only in the mode of *technology (Zuhandenheit)*. The intention in the next section is to show how the uncanny joy of nothing experiences may reveal themselves and elevate from technology and rigid practice of equipmentality.

Anxiety and nothing in educational practice

(7) The case study we have conducted is primarily a contribution to context-dependent knowledge. As mentioned in the methods chapter, we believe at any rate that we have hopefully helped to make our "findings" and analyses applicable to others by both the practice-oriented approach and through our frankness about the challenges, pitfalls and various real circumstances we have encountered in the "collision" between theory and practice. It is our opinion, therefore, that our findings, analyses and deliberations are transferable to other contexts. Each year, there are a large number of externally initiated

development programmes that must be accepted, "translated", legitimised and integrated in Norwegian municipalities. Our research and experience can thus serve as a small contribution to both theory and practice development for agents and managers of change in municipalities other than our own. According to Irgens (2011), (knowledge) management must be primarily not only practice-oriented and pragmatic but also knowledge-based. This is a reality that we can acknowledge. As we have displayed for the reader, these perspectives are not yet fully interwoven and integrated into our mindsets and our actions. We have done much reflection *about* action. We have not quite crossed the finish line in terms of reflecting *in* action. Nevertheless, we feel that we are well on our way!

Technology is reflected in the fact that "our findings, analyses and deliberations are transferable to other contexts"; that is to say, our findings, analyses and deliberations can be ordered and are ready for use. However, the vignette also reveals a certain incompleteness in the sense that there are still "pitfalls" and a potential notion of nothingness, while at the same time it is claimed that "these perspectives are not yet fully interwoven and integrated into our mindsets and our actions". Being-there (Da-sein) reveals its quality here, that is to say, that there is constantly something still to be settled. (cf. what I refer to later in the chapter as Being-reserved). In the next vignette, reference is made to an additional aspect of a newly acquired understanding.

(8) The journey has brought me to places in the world of knowledge that I didn't know existed and that I have become better acquainted with. I have also become better acquainted with new aspects of myself; I have become more reflective, I see things in multiple and different perspectives, and I still have more to learn. Fortunately, having to relate to multiple perspectives in my reflections has challenged the framework for understanding, and I have discovered connections and challenges that I have absorbed as part of the knowledge development that I have taken part in – and am still a part of.

The student states that he/she has "*become acquainted with new aspects of myself*", which, in a post-rationalisation light, might be interpreted as the discovery of a new being-in-the-world, a new home in the form of new "places in the world of knowledge" that might also be regarded as entailing a new familiarity with a new language play. The declared connection between a new world of knowledge and a different acquaintance with myself may mean, in other words, an encounter with nothingness, in terms of the notion that Nothing appears to be *holding* or *swaying* amongst beings (i.e. "multiple perspectives") and *allowing* new beings and self-understanding to be. The next vignette also focuses attention on the significance of (theorised) reflection and the potential for a new self – nothing-understanding.

> (9) One of the objectives of the master's degree in knowledge management is to become a reflecting practitioner. I had thought I already was one. I was wrong. I reflected before, as well, but through the study, reflection has changed; it has become more theoretical, more primary, and it has created and continues to create knowledge that I take along on my journey into the world of knowledge.
>
> As an introduction to the thesis, I cited an extract from the poem "Finally free" by Anne Elisabeth Lien that I came across some years ago. I found the poem touching at the time, and I still do. Therefore, I will end by quoting the poem in its entirety:
>
> **Finally free**
>
> *I have begun to fly, not*
> *high but I have left the nest.*
> *I have sought the world outside, not*
> *Lonely, but nevertheless alone*
> *I have begun to learn, am*
> *not fully trained but*
> *manage on my own nonetheless I have set out on*
> *the journey through the rest of my life, am*
> *unafraid, but simply thankful.*
>
> It is now that my learning process commences. It is now that the journey can truly begin. I am thankful and I am looking forward to it.

The claim that "reflection has changed; it has become more theoretical" may show a (problematic) assumption at the heart of such approaches: the *primacy of the theoretical*. The entire problematic has arrived at a crucial point, which, however, appears insignificant. In light of the poem, we may induce that there is an abyss: either into nothingness or "*we somehow leap into another world, more precisely, we manage for the first time to make the leap into the world as such*" (Heidegger, 2000a, p. 51).

Being-there (the student) is always ahead of itself or in the students' perspective, "*It is now that my learning process begins. It is now that the trip truly begins*". So, being-there is understood in terms of possibilities. What is most primordial is neither the students-as-researchers nor research objects, but rather the "nothing" in which specific (theoretical) forms of (post)student existence go along with a new life-project, an emerging route of *possibilities* or leap-into-presence.

---

(10) Our reflections over the learning process

Our process leading up to the conclusion of the thesis had a strong impact on us, both personally and professionally. The fact that we have been two researchers has been demanding and inspiring. We experienced that informal, incoherent and oftentimes chaotic conversations helped to bring out new insights, which in turn urged us onward. The conversations were not preplanned, other than that we planned to meet together. Many times we would look at one another and ask: How are we going to do this? We always wound up starting, and doing something different than what we had suggested to one another. In hindsight, we said we had accomplished something smart that made us advance, but it was always something other than what we anticipated beforehand.

They experience difficulties when faced with an indeterminate research situation, in which they cannot at first make out *what* it is that is important to them. Indeterminateness explicated as the term horizon (cf. Chapter 1) may describe the indeterminate nature and always already existing potential of nothing, which includes some form of passive compulsion; hence expressions like "*other than what we could see beforehand*" or paraphrased like "We do not decide our experiences ourselves!?" Perhaps the students could say, "experiences force themselves on us!" This enforced indeterminateness and aspect of nothing are further illustrated in a radical way in the statement: "*Higher than actuality stands possibility*" (Heidegger, 1962, p. 38). Students are thus initiated into a practice by learning to enact relevant distinctions in their research process, with each new experience enlarging one's "grammatical" (Wittgenstein, 1953) sense. In the next vignette, the presence of the "grammatical" and projection sense show up again.

(11) Demanding and exciting . . . Darsø and Brearly (2008, p. 639) say that working with artistic expressions in organisations demands courage, trust and a will to walk the narrow path/move along the sharp ridge. This is not mainstream work, and it is not always safe. Pioneer work of this nature, particularly in finding a context, requires a rare sensitivity to the context itself and a deep knowledge of one's own strengths and limits, combined with a strong theoretical foundation.

It has been a demanding and exciting task to work with, but it has been well worth the effort. One challenge I want to emphasise, however, is that of our experiences with methodology. I have found this particularly difficult. For a long time, I had thought that what I wanted, was supposed to use and had to use was an action-based methods approach, and I struggled terribly to get a grasp on what that really was. Eventually, I became aware that there were particular monotypes and the process surrounding them that caused my confusion. By having read theory about both art and method, I can say, on the one hand, that monotype is a processing tool that can sometimes be used not only as an art object in and of itself but also as an object for conversation and reflection. At the same time, it is a methodical and scientific action-based tool that can be characterised as a reflection-in-action. This means that it is an expression for systematic observation that is given expression while observation is ongoing. I don't know yet what it actually entails, but I am convinced that precisely because it is at the same time an art object, an object of conversation and reflection, a scientific tool and method, it has a potential that can be further developed. This is a trail I would like to follow.

When the student writes about monotype as a tool, a basic uncertainty is underscored: "*I don't know yet what it actually entails, . . . (but it has a potential that can be further developed*". This is followed by the utterance "A trail I would like to follow", which points to the fact that the student is thus initiated into a practice by learning to enact relevant distinctions in practice, with each new experience enlarging one's *grammatical* (Wittgenstein, 1953) sense of what the proper usage is (i.e. monotype as a processing tool), namely, the sense of what in the future can *possibly* follow on from her hitherto experiences. Nothing-at-home utterances such as "*it isn't always safe*" and "*I struggled terribly to get a grasp on what it was*" are also reflected in the next vignette.

(12) I elevated day-to-day meetings and turned them into art; by doing that, I put them in a totally special and different light. I was involved in creating daily magic, which I believe is an important contribution that artists can make to organisations. If we are allowed to contribute, and if people dare to take a different vantage point so that they can begin to accept that there is intelligence behind what is happening, even without understanding it, more people will experience days of daily magic that will be long remembered. Art-based thinking means taking the individual's inherent will and creative power seriously, but it is also a matter of being people who listen and are present in relation to themselves and others. To be a creative person is a matter of understanding that one must be present in *transientness*, the state in which art and aesthetics can render the invisible visible in precisely the same manner as *The lonely chair,* in a momentary encounter, was seen through a temperament.

The words "*be present in transientness*" which "*can render the invisible visible*" is a reference to the art of not having a firm grip, or in other words, not being at home in a familiar world but daring to be temporarily lost in an inhospitable nothing-sphere. Perhaps it is a matter of being grasped before grasping in an unforeseen way (new conception). To put it differently, in this way, anxiety supposedly makes manifest Nothing as part of the background against which entities are intelligible, that is something that "*can make the invisible visible*" and help one to "*take a different vantage point*". It may help to paraphrase Wittgenstein's words in order to provide insight, namely, to look at things as if seeing them for the very first time (cf. Wittgenstein's perspective of wonder, see Chapter 5). Perhaps the ability to see something right before our eyes in a new way can be applied to students' understanding of data and the significance of transcribing.

(13) Transcription took a tremendous amount of time and was the heaviest phase of the research process, while at the same time it gave us enormous insight into the data. The tough job of working our way out of this phase took us in several different directions. The joy in eventually finding our way was great. It is the *road* to the goal that was the greatest source of learning. Particularly when time began to run out and we saw through maturation and new learning what we might be able to do differently.

These two students come to *Gelassenheit* through an occasion of letting-themselves-in (Heidegger, 1966); that is to say, they dwell or let themselves, in transcription, practise as "the heaviest phase of the research process". This view of the amount of data is accompanied by a lack of precise knowledge as to what they are searching for (findings, possible interpretations, potential analysis, categories of data, etc.). This is not a matter of representation; it is by being immersed in the uncanny "conversation" of not-being-at-home anymore. The experience of such a "transcription" thinking is in waiting without waiting for a particular outcome; it is not the result of a fully formed intention to search for a predetermined concept (i.e. a deductive research strategy) but something that emerges along the way (Unterwegs) or "on the path towards the goal" (the goal being interpreted as the completed thesis). In retrospective mode, they perhaps see more clearly how this project "took us in several different directions" and contributed towards acquiring "new learning" in the form of an understanding "of what we might imagine we could have done differently". This indicates an understanding towards the *for-the-sake-of-which*, that is Dasein (being-there) gaining access to self-understanding (Heidegger, 1962). This may point towards how students at first might understand themselves and their research process differently. As such:

---

(14) For us, this practical wisdom was a matter of general wondering about our own ability to act and reason, a realisation that can help to establish new routines in our work as leaders. By *not* claiming that we had all the answers, but instead seeking to create a corresponding wondering about them, we can help the individual to continue his/her own Socratic self-education. If we had returned with the answers, the flames of wonderment would presumably have died out. We should see to it that this basic wondering – or reflection about praxis – does not die out when we now return to our day-to-day work as instructors or advisers for the future leaders at the Royal Norwegian Air Force Academy.

The importance of "a general wondering" in pedagogical practice is asserted here. In other words, it is not only "reflection about praxis" and "practical wisdom" in pedagogical praxis but also an existential mode, or the "basic wondering" that challenges our way of being-in-the-world. Moreover, this (nothing) pedagogy may be further elaborated with Heidegger's 1951–1952 account of teaching and learning:

Teaching is even more difficult than learning. We know that; but we rarely think about it. And why is teaching more difficult than learning? Not because the teacher must have a larger store of information, and have it always ready. Teaching is more difficult than learning because what teaching calls for is this: to let learn. The real teacher, in fact, lets nothing else be learned than – learning. His conduct, therefore, often produces the impression that we properly learn nothing from him, if by "learning" we now suddenly understand merely the procurement of useful information. The teacher is ahead of his apprentices in this alone, that he has still far more to learn than they – he has to learn to let them learn.

(Heidegger, 1968, p. 15)

The next vignette perhaps shows precisely the importance of "*to learn to let them learn*".

---

(15) On the personal level, the thesis has been a *great* contribution to my own development and maturation. For example, I have learnt that I am much "squarer" mentally than I had thought at the outset. What has frustrated me most in the work, and what I have found most difficult to tackle, was the initial period when things were still unclarified and I didn't know where I was headed with the thesis. Conversely, it was a great joy and relief to find my way out of the "fog" and onto the road, with a map spread out beside me. From that point on, and all the way to my destination, it was often a good feeling, like cruising along a motorway with the music turned up full volume, interrupted only with quick glances at the map to ensure that I was going in the right direction. But at times, usually abruptly and without warning, the fog rolled in and settled over the equipage once again, and the map blew away in the wind, and I had to come to a screeching halt, take detours and conduct turnaround operations. What I am most proud of is that I indeed managed to find my way; I managed to turn chaos into order and to plan, time and again. Not entirely alone, admittedly, I had good helpers along the way, but nevertheless: it was I who did the job. Because I think that this aspect of the work was the most difficult to handle: the frustration and impatience I felt at having lost my way and lost the map, several times, it is this that has taught me most on the personal level.

This vignette illustrates a student *en route* (unterwegs) with the master's thesis, articulated particularly by the statement *"usually abruptly and without warning, the fog rolled in and settled over the equipage once again, and the map blew away in the wind, and I had to come to a screeching halt"*. *"The screeching halt"* signals a being-there that lives-though the experience of Nothing. When a student being is found in this state, the being supposedly slides back under the pressure of an increasing *meaninglessness*; they become unimportant and disconnected from their fitting jointness (*the map*) and are left to slide beneath their concernfully meaningful places in the world. (This is what I term *being blank* later in this chapter.) Moreover, the utterance *"frustration and impatience at losing, up to several times, both one's way and the map"* points to the uncanny feeling (angst) of not-being-at-home anymore. Or, as it is more poetically phrased in Hamsun's work *The Road Leads On* (Men livet lever):

> *He, the protagonist, August, sits here between his ears and hears true emptiness. Quite amusing, a fancy. On the ocean something stirred, and there, there was a sound, something audible, a water chorus. Here nothing meets nothing and is not there, there is not even a hole. One can only shake one's head in resignation.*

> (quoted in Heidegger, 2000b, p. 29)

The fog and the sound of the ocean waves symbolise an experience of homelessness and a temporary being-dormant or withdrawal of being feeling. In other words, such a lack of totality signifies that there is something still outstanding in the students potentiality-for-Being:

---

(16) "Couldn't see the forest for the trees"

Through the study programme, I have had two "slaps in the face" in terms of my relationship with my own workplace and the survey. It is hard for me to express in words what was important to investigate at Havo. I became emotional in the way I expressed myself and it was difficult for my partner, as well as my adviser, to grasp what I meant to say. Perhaps I wasn't completely aware of it myself, beyond the fact that I felt a premonition? I saw in hindsight that I probably lacked distanciation from my own field of work. Without Marit's perspective as an outsider in terms of Havo, it would have been difficult for me to distance myself enough to create a study with a research topic, hypothesis and research questions. I realise that the Nordland Research Report and its findings were also a contribution.

> Even though I had read about the challenges to conducting research when it involves one's own, I still failed to see the consequences of it before I experienced it personally. In the absence of a patient and wise fellow student, the thesis would never have seen the light of day.

Although not the deepest form of Nothing, but something similar, is indicated with phrases like "*difficult to express in words*" but "*I had a premonition*". Clearly, components such as "*research issue, hypothesis and research questions*" are not prepared in advance or are ready-to-order but are created on the way to nothing. The utterances, "It is hard for me to express in words what was important to investigate at Havo. I became emotional in the way I expressed myself and it was difficult for my partner as well as my adviser to grasp what I meant to say", suggest a nothing mode characterised by language playing second violin in being-in-the-world.

The expression, "*couldn't see the forest for the trees*", demonstrates a Nothing-experience which escapes the measures of being-there (existence), and being-there is "at the mercy" of Nothing, without being able fully to know whence Nothing came upon it, or whether Nothing has *totally* uncovered its potential with the help of the there *(Da)* of Being-there *(Da-sein)*. In the existential mode of experiencing anxiety (i.e. *Until I experienced it personally*), Nothing simply "drags" being-there in its *there*. The next vignette expresses a similar experience of nothing and not-being-at-home.

> (17) I have found it challenging to persevere through processes, and I have benefited from Senge and Argyris' lefthand-column exercise, which encourages the participant to put thoughts and feelings into words that are parallel with the uttered words in a conversation. We haven't begun to use this exercise in NAV telephone conversations, but I have used it myself to some extent after having had conversations and brief meetings after which I have *felt it in the pit of my stomach* and later pondered the somewhat non-constructive question *What am I doing?* I have had the pleasure (and felt the excitement and groping) when trying out work methods and techniques in collaboration with an engaged group of leaders and a fantastic group of employees.

The statement, "*Senge og Argyris' lefthand-column exercise, which encourages the participant to put thoughts and feelings into words that are parallel with the uttered words in a conversation*", points to an appropriated language game. This activity and the language game are used when the "somewhat non-constructive question" *What am I doing?* pops up. The question derives from a Nothing-experience characterised by the lack of helpful equipment that does not always emerge in every situation (Being-slow).

Thus, the student comes to experience certain situations (i.e. "After conversations and minor meetings") initially as difficulties, to the extent that she has already come to embody certain expectations, anticipations and projections as a consequence of certain ways of being and doing things. It is when the flow of her work is disrupted and she became disoriented (i.e. "what am I doing?"), not knowing how next to "go on" (Wittgenstein, 1953), that she faces a difficulty, which may be engulfed with projections (possibilities) later illustrated by "Senge and Argyris' lefthand-column game". On second thought, it is perhaps the case that both the question and the "answer" (lefthand column exercise) are parts of the same language game since the meaning of the question and its "use" is, as Wittgenstein (1953, I, sec. 43) says: "*the meaning of a word is its use in the language*". If the question and the words do not eventually become meaning bearers, there are then grounds to speak of a more comprehensively uncanny experience of nothingness.

Remarks on vignettes

Since the understanding is thus constantly torn away from nothing and into technology, the movement or aspects of nothing may be characterised *in different ways*. So, then, is it possible to see patterns in nothing experiences? Examples and vignettes suggest that students are involved in different "nothing" experiences, that is from their life as the avoidance practice (keeping nothing away) to the severe loss of the taken-for-granted way of being-in-the-world. Based on this material, I will describe four ways in which students may "suffer" and take advantage of the nothing experience: (1) Being-reserved, (2) Being-slow, (3) Being-blank and (4) Being-ecstatic.

(1) Being-reserved

This equipmentality (i.e. "learning outcome" and all the vignettes from 1 to 7) illustrates a way of being-reserved or technology-being. Although hermeneutic in principle and always already open for possibilities is its ability to close off other potential effective forms of understanding, education and pedagogies. Despite its disclosing historical unfoldings, Being as Being or Being in its mysterious universality (that Heidegger aspires to explore and what Wittgenstein calls wonder) has never unfolded the entirety of its possible disclosures within the epochs of history. There is always already a not-yet-disclosed "reserve" of it that has not yet come to its truth. The phenomena for this kind of unavailability, *concealment or* absent-mindedness are always there in a blurred sense. There is a sense in which Being as Being always remains in *radical* retreat or what I call Being-reserved.

(2) Being-slow

Being-slow involves the students slowing down activity (i.e. lack of theoretical, analytical, empirical, methodological skills) until it becomes halting and there is a potential for a remote uncanniness. Such a phenomenon may be seen in vignettes 11, 13 and 16. This disclosed Being as sense supposedly becomes a slow phenomenon in students' experiences in the context of the *problematic* confrontation with equipment. We may also assume that this forgetfulness (Vergessenhet) can become the subject matter of a potential wondering student. This Being is disclosed as the current historical worldliness, even though it may not yet be manifestly or thematically evident, a fully appearing and grasped educational phenomenon.

(3) Being-blank

It seems that Being-blank may have two effects:

1   *Angst* makes students flee from themselves and take refuge in, or "fall into", familiar intraworldly things; that is to say, a kind of technological familiar being.
2   Occasional, explicit *Angst* rips students away from the familiar and discloses bare Being-there (Dasein) and its bare world. Explicit *Angst* serves the student in two ways: (a) in general, it reveals being-there in its unity; (b) the student's *own Angst* detaches her from worldly concerns and prejudices, making education possible. Such aspects of being-blank are discussed in vignettes 8, 12, 14 and 15. Overall, in nothing as anxiety, students have the experience of the whole of beings but, again, as a whole that slips away. Thus, what is left is the bare structure of being-there (Da-sein), a bare world, a net Being-in-the-world without the usual accompaniments.

(4) Being-ecstatic

Being-ecstatic may serve as an objection to those who "merely" make students (or other educational participants) the centre, without recognising that making students the centre, makes *the nothingness of the centre the fundamental problem*. Heidegger's (1962) insight may be helpful here: Let it be granted that students are "the centre". Since students are nothingness, the centre is nothingness, and this means that *being-there* must be *ecstatic* or "excentric". Since the "excentric" is that which is *off-centre*, this means that the ontological way of being assigned to an educational substantial centre *must shift to the periphery* (off-centre). Thus, *Being-there* turns out to be "centred", not in some mental cognitive activity or internal psychological processes (as stated by many learning theories, cf. Chapter 3) but in the former periphery, the shared public world or language games. This "excentric" character is just what Heidegger (1962) means by saying that *Being-there's* Being is Being-in-the-world. Moreover, since this means there is nothingness at the centre, one must re-conceptualise the centre as *ecstatic* or "excentric", which turns one's understanding of Being and students' existence upside down. Maybe this turning of one's understanding is most clearly seen in vignettes 9 and 17.

Ways of nothing-in-the-educational world

Thus, there are certain special kinds of involved, uncanny passive, nothing *encounters* which, when they occur, may give rise to distinctive feelings within the students (i.e. not-being-at-home). And it is these feelings aroused in students by the "passive" movements of (Nothing) that enable them to maybe reveal something of the unique nature of our "inner world" or way of being. It is this kind of "movements" of the nothing "within us" – as they with indirect lightning express their significance – that is, the sleek passivity of the contours of nothing, so to speak, of *their* living of their lives. But this only becomes accessible to students in what we might call our *engaged* meetings with them, involvements in which they truly respect their otherness, their difference from our being.

Just as we may have a felt sense that someone across a room is deliberately not looking at us, or, that someone we are talking to at a party has "faded away and left us", and is looking over our shoulder for their next port of call. At this moment, it is the sense of "without us", in a way, that may be special for us, that makes us feel disconnected or not-at-home in a way that matters, that makes a difference to us. Similarly with all these students, they also (I surmise) had a felt sense that the Nothing was at that moment "with" them in a way that was special for them. As I see it, in all these (reserved, slow, blank and ecstatic) nothing episodes, as I put it, the Nothing before us is a nothingness that enters into us and makes us a (potential) other educational being.

Something very special occurs when student beings meet and begin to *respond* to each other and in the situation of nothing (more happens than them merely having an *impact* on each other). In such nothing meetings, the creation of quite novel and distinct language games which, more than merely average technological forms, are themselves spheres or unities within which students can then become both immersed and blank. And what is very special about such indirect liminal lightning spheres – those exemplified above as *being-slow, being-blank* – is that just like the other persons around us, they have *passivity* in the sense that they can exert a forceful influence on us, but not like the direct activity and impact of physical force, but instead the absence of both another person's and one's own *expressions*, by not being sensitive or in the mood to "calls" or "demands" in the situation. If this (responsive) engagement with the other beings and our own being and nothing is lost, then our access to what uniquely matters to us in our "inner lives" is lost too. This is what is at stake.

A dominant technological education and psychotics have something in common; they cannot tolerate gaps because any gap becomes totally overpowering; it is where the nothing of the being gets through and is frozen. This is why, for example, when you speak to a psychotic, they are certain about everything – everything is connected and has a meaning related to their delusion. These vignettes show that there are many gaps or aspects of nothing that unwarrantedly pop up from the technological educational systems, and perhaps good higher education and scholastic achievements rest upon how these nothing experiences are dealt with.

Notes

1 The admission criteria for this two-year and nine-month-long seminar and part-time-based master's degree programme (90 credits in knowledge management) places emphasis on non-formal qualifications. At least two years' relevant occupational practice that, in this context, documents competence in the field of leadership and organisation. It might be added that most of the students have many more years of relevant occupational practice. This means that the students largely have comprehensive experience and knowledge about the way different sectors of working life function; the students also come from both the public (ca. 80%) and the private (ca. 20%) sector. This may be of significance because better conditions are laid for teaching, advising and learning that are dependent on actors with very different practical experiences and theoretical backgrounds talking together and collaborating on the master's thesis, often towards the end of the study programme (very few students write the thesis alone). According to the student barometer (www.studiebarometeret.no/no/student/studieprogram/1174_90mkl/), this study programme has for many years been one of the highest scored in Norway in terms of the overall student satisfaction when compared with other economic/administrative subjects. This high

score is possibly due to the fact that the students are regularly challenged, and challenge themselves, in the tension between (academic/scientific) theory and (personal) praxis and experience, entailing that uncanny and homeless perceptions of nothing occur that may contribute towards a new self-understanding and enhanced learning.

2 These terms are chosen in light of how they may illuminate the data/vignettes and not at least how they may co-work with the term and main phenomena of nothing. Of course, one important factor is also my understanding of how Heideggerian and Wittgensteinian concepts may illuminate each other. The affinities between Heidegger and Wittgenstein can be enlarged with several other parallel terms, that is event (Ereignis)-the genesis of language.

References

Ardra (Eds.). *Handbook of arts in qualitative research: perspectives, methodologies, and issues.* California: SAGE.

Darsø, L. & Brearley, L. (2008). Business studies: vivifying data and experience through artful approaches. G.J. Knowles and A. L.

Heidegger, H. (1977). The Question Concerning Technology. In W. Lovitt (Ed.), *The Question Concerning Technology and Other Essays.* New York: Harper & Row Publishers.

Heidegger, M. (1962). *Being and Time.* New York: Harper & Row Publishers.

Heidegger, M. (1966). Conversation on a Country Path about Thinking. In M. Heidegger (Ed.), *Discourse on Thinking* (J. M. Anderson & E. H. Freund, Trans.). New York: Harper and Row.

Heidegger, M. (1968). *What is Called Thinking?* (F. D. Wieck & J. G. Gray, Trans.). New York: Harper Collins.

Heidegger, M. (2000a). *Introduction to Metaphysics* (G. Fried & R. Polt, Trans.). London: Yale University Press.

Heidegger, M. (2000b). *Zur Bestimmung der Philosophie* (B. Heimbüchel, Ed.). Frankfurt am Main: V. Klostermann, 1987. Translated by T. Sadler, *Towards the Definition of Philosophy.* London: The Athlone Press.

Irgens, E. J. (2011). Dynamiske og lærende organisasjoner. Bergen: Fagbokforlaget.

Johnson, D. W., & Johnson, R. T. (1991). *Learning Together and Alone: Cooperative, Competitive, and Individualistic* (3rd ed.). Englewood Cliffs, NJ: Prentice Hall.

OECD. (2012). Retrieved from www.oecd.org/education/skills-beyond-school/AHELOFSReportVolume1.pdf

Rehn, A., & Taalas, S. (2009). On Wittgenstein and Management at Rest: Prolegomena to a Philosophy of Problems. *Philosophy of Management,* (7), pp. 89–95.

Rennemo, Ø., & Vaag, J. R. (2018). Collective Leadership Learning (CLL) – Leader Reflections on Learning During Higher-Level, Experience-based Leadership Education. *Scandinavian Psychologist,* 5, e13. https://doi.org/10.15714/scandpsychol.5.e13

Wittgenstein, L. (1953). *Philosophische Untersuchungen* (Translated as *Philosophical Investigations* [in German and English], Rev. 4th ed., by G. E. M. Anscombe,

P. M. S. Hacker, & J. Schulte). Chichester, West Sussex, UK and Malden, MA: Wiley-Blackwell, 2009.

Wittgenstein, L. (1969). *On Certainty* (G. E. M. Anscombe and G. H. von Wright, Eds.; D. P. Paul and G. E. M. Anscombe, Trans.). Oxford: Blackwell.

Wittgenstein, L. (1977). *Remarks on Color.* Berkeley: University of California Press.

Wittgenstein, L. (1980). *Culture and Value* (G. H. Von Wright & H. Nyman, Eds.; P. Winch, Trans.). Chicago, IL: The University of Chicago Press.

Wittgenstein, L. (2005). *Tractacus Logico Philosophicus.* London: Routledge.

8 Implications and reflections on nothing for educational theory, research and practice

This chapter proposes implications of nothing for educational theory, research and practice. Nothing may invite too many implications, but here I delineate potential consequences for fertile points of view, the everyday language and theory; how research education focuses non-critically on "too early and too late" aspects that otherwise are undercommunicated; and how nothing may work or not work in practice.

Implications for theory

Raynes and Rutledge (2010) make an intriguing comment: "*The purpose of academic life is not to learn laundry lists by heart but, on the contrary, to be able to reason from the ground up*" (p. 290). In their view, only from such a ground-up approach can "*finance understand itself out of itself*" (p. 457), and we might add, only from such (groundless) ground can education understand itself out of itself. With regard to the status of theory or conceptual abstractions, the theory in use depends on the end of the social science, the craft or the action, as well as on the subject matter of investigation: "*it is a mark of the trained mind never to expect more precision in the treatment of any subject than the nature of that subject permits*" (Aristotle, 1988, pp. 63 and 65).

With these words in mind, it is possible to argue against defining inquiry as the search for the appropriate unit of analysis, because I think that a unit of analysis has to be specific to a particular inquiry and the material at hand. I think the unit of analysis in social science or humanities research should not be totalising and comprehensive but rather contextual, sensitive to nothingness and should stick to the thing in itself (die Sache selbst). Having said all this, I have found Heidegger and Wittgenstein's approach to nothingness and wonder to be their potential totalising unit of "analysis" of nothing promising and certainly underestimated and that we may borrow without (nothing) concerns from the dominant non-nothing tradition of

DOI: 10.4324/9781003222231-10

projection and grammar capacity, being-in-the-world and language game (cf. Chapters 6 and 7).

Perhaps we endeavour always to (theoretically, methodologically and empirically) explain and thereby convince ourselves, perhaps unwittingly, that the educational mystery of things is somehow no longer there. As soon as one adopts a matter-of-fact, explanatory posture towards the phenomena under investigation, whether in the form of evidence or an effect-based approach or an inviolable theory (i.e. dogmatic use of socio-cultural views), one often sacrifices the capacity to be in awe of those phenomena.

What if educational science is a source of impoverishment because one particular theory or method elbows all others aside. As a consequence, they all seem paltry by comparison, preliminary stages at best. Why no yendeavour to go to the original sources so as to see them all side by side, both the neglected and the preferred. The result would be an "enrichment" through the multiplication of "fertile new points of view" (cf. Wittgenstein's, 1953 term of Übersicht). What if the overvaluation of the empirical and the under-valuation of the "grammatical" (i.e. fertile new points of view) have led us into theoretical and methodological dead-end streets and to a minimally applicable practical pedagogy.

Pedagogical terminology is quite commonly developed from everyday language. One direct consequence of this is that pedagogical hypotheses easily become pseudo-empirical, that is to say, we test hypotheses that necessarily result from interdependent relationships between the words that are used. It should be added that pedagogical research has frequently used terms that are not defined clearly, and it is therefore taken for granted that the connection between them must be studied empirically. Example: research showing empirically that teaching leads to learning, without one's having reflected over whether the term learning logically presupposes teaching (in an educational context). No one can learn without having been taught! Another example: we know that the student's learning behaviour and the teacher's teaching must be goal-oriented. This is obvious because language presupposes it. Examples such as these articulate what we know about ourselves prior to all experience and which structures everything we experience.

By analysing our (pedagogical) language, however, we can more clearly see what we already implicitly know, as well as our possibilities for perceiving, experiencing, understanding and predicting. It is challenging to alter or exceed our basic form of understanding because it is already given in the ways we perceive, act and report. Couched in the terminology of Jean Piaget (1953), it might be said that one cannot accommodate something that is not assimilated. Based on taking the phenomenon of nothing seriously, it is possible to see possibilities (projections) that do not primarily crystallise as increased knowledge and ways of knowing, but rather in ways of being-nothing and realisations of existence (which underlie the logical relation between assimilation and accommodation).

Instead of building upon empirically based qualitative and quantitative research and theories, learning outcome manuals and skills regimes, the alternative is to analyse and perhaps rearrange what already exists (always already) and which is partially built into the language and rests on a way of being, and which I choose here to call a praxis of nothingness. It is the grounds for a praxis in which pedagogy functions phenomenologically (cf. Chapter 5), that is, he or she meets the student/pupil and himself/herself with the most unbiased openness possible and experiences working in collaboration with the other and linguistic tangles.

What if educational problems are not empirical problems but are instead dissolved, by looking into the workings of our language, and in such a way as to make us recognise those workings, in spite of an urge to misunderstand them. The problems are dissolved, not by giving new information, new data, new evidence, new theories and curriculum plans but by "arranging" what we have always known. It is tempting to creatively paraphrase Wittgenstein (1953); education is a battle against the bewitchment of our intelligence by means of language (§109). As such, there is a chance, in education, of saying everything without touching upon the secret of nothing.

Implications for research

The theory of Nothing may show that as we (re-)search for grounding and methodology (how to proceed in (phenomenological) research practice, for example), the researcher must inevitably encounter being itself as non-being, non-presence, nothingness. As the researcher searches for a constant presence in which to ground herself, she may ultimately arrive at absence, which inevitably resists her attempts. The being which she encounters is not grounding, but rather an abyss, in the face of which thinking-in-search-of-grounding efforts remain futile. Here, there is a radical point of view, this abyss (being), may indeed be the ultimate purpose of thinking and way of doing (phenomenological) research.

Within the boundaries of research resting on hermeneutical reflection, we invariably pose questions about some whole (Gadamer, 1960). However, science studies a select discipline of reality or, in stronger terms, a specific sliver of being. A theory of nothing-immersed research, by contrast, thrives in a sense on the basis of what is not; it derives its meaning from nothingness. The research method applied by the "nothing" researcher is known as the "hermeneutic circle", one that more disciplined minds refer to as a "vicious circle". It begins by assuming what it sets out to prove. For

Heidegger (1962) and Wittgenstein (1953), there is no such thing as pure thought. In researching, tracing and thinking, we rely on many assumptions and terms, including those of which we are still attempting to demonstrate the validity (see Chapter 3). It is important to be reminded that Nothing cannot be predicated and systematically evoked, because Nothing is the *nothing and nowhere* that comes about by the trivialisation of worldly beings. Hence, this does not exclude positivistic, "active" and purposeful (research) questions like "Where shall we seek the nothing? Where will we find the nothing?" In order to find something, mustn't we already know in advance (in some way) that it is there? At first and for the most part, the researcher can seek only when he has anticipated the being at hand of what he is looking for. Now the nothing *is* what we are seeking. This might work but has in principle nothing to do with Nothing (cf. the six pivotal aspects in Chapter 1).

However, following the positivistic line, what "is" it, this essence of actively seeking nothing? Heidegger and Wittgenstein equate it with experiences of wonder, strangeness, anxiety, not-being-at-home, as the complete negation of the totality of beings. It is because of "the nothing" that one senses that a being cannot be wholly encapsulated, as such a "depiction" would inevitably have to account for its expiration and disintegration, and with it, its indeterminate and uncanny nothingness. We relate to being, we experience it at the moment it reveals itself to us. This is the state of *Dasein*, "being-there" (Heidegger, 1962) and "wonder" Wittgenstein (1953). This state may occur vis-à-vis the nothing but rarely enough and only for a moment.

The researcher may experience the nothing as a sense of anxiety, different from fear, which is itself "fear in the face of" something. Anxiety is not associated with anything, or more aptly, it is associated with Nothing. An existential experience of the incomprehensibility of existence (i.e. collapsed research projects), of the vacuum that we attempt to fill with "compulsive talk" (i.e. nothing "covered up" or transformed in claims of validity, reliability, researcher-as-instrument), as the nothing is a way of robbing us of genuine speech.

To summarise: to the (cartesian) analytical, distanced and calculative researcher who seeks secure ground at all costs (i.e. trying to override and overlook being too early and too late, see further explanation in the following), nothingness is impossibility. It is beyond their comprehension and cannot resonate and be "voiced" explicitly in a research text. It thus becomes "unutterable, inexpressible, unintelligible". So, at the backdrop of a theory of nothing, the more forcefully and cleverly some researchers strive to refute the claim of the nonexistence of nothingness, the more they contradict themselves (as they refer to it, in the very act of refutation, as something that exists). Thus, the researcher who ascribes to existent things a pinch of nonexistence commits unwarranted attribution, a reprehensible offense against methodological practice in social science. There are "too early and late" paths one is not advised or allowed to follow (at least not as a written research(ing) text).

This is a matter of what often slips away in practical research. It is what belatedly or never allows itself to be captured in language, what we can only sense the importance of and the meaning of (pre-anticipated), but that eludes the clear and sharp scrutiny of the researcher along with the researcher's conceptualisation. What slips away and vanishes may subsequently be forgotten forever or be clad in language that is more crystal clear than the phenomenon itself. The concept (theory) and the phenomenon may be two sides of the same coin, but they needn't be. For example, it is doubtful that grades sufficiently reflect a student's understanding of the subject matter.

In research, it is challenging to bestow on the object of research a "fair" language and relevant/reliable terms. Part of this challenge is a question of the relationships and the journey between (dead) terms/theories/abstractions and concrete experiences. Neither theory/concepts nor concrete experiences last very long on their own in the research process before the real and necessary dynamics begin to fade. It is impossible to manage without concepts, theories and abstractions in research, but the essential thing is the way they return to living experiences. This does not mean that everything can be conceptualised and that theories can exhaust all facets of a given phenomenon. One main premise is to remain aware that the totality of what we are attempting to research eludes our conceptual capacity and aptitude. As Whitehead (1938, p. 124) expresses the connection between abstractions and "living experience", "*The return may be misconceived. The abstraction may misdirect us as the real complexity from which it originates*".

Some of these "method-less" and "incommunicable" experiences are frequently the ones that for various reasons do not fit into the research project and dissertation's chapter on theory and methodology. They are experiences that do not come into their own until they are couched in language, meaning that they are understood and underscored, for example, in the methodology text itself, and not until the actual choices of methods and assessment criteria have been made. This may be a kind of post-rationalisation that is indeed quite common, because the rationale for methodological practice and (unconscious) choices emerge much more clearly after major portions of the research have been completed. To put it another way, as a researcher, you missed the boat. In a sense, it might be claimed that (qualitative) researchers always miss the boat.

It is possible that the significance of the inherent dimension of "Nothingness" in qualitative research may be highly underestimated. It is a matter of the researcher's existential options/limitations that frequently underlie or precede the established methodological and theoretical accessways. In one sense, it might be said that the researcher's existential realisations are seldom explicated in research texts and publications and that they may often remain concealed and difficult for the researcher to put into words. Polanyi's (2002) well-known adage that *we know more than we can tell* applies to researchers as well. Somehow, existence (the potential for new realisations of existence or self-understanding) *always come to light too late*.

It is perhaps true that an a priori understanding as a methods perspective may, to a disproportionately large extent, hide accessways leading to the researcher's own possibilities. Qualitative a priori or predetermined methods that maintain their privileged access to practice possibly have a tendency to ignore unscrutinised options and "living experiences" that are already present. This applies not only to the objects of research but also to the researcher's own understanding of herself and her practical research possibilities.

Van Manen (1989) states that, "*A Human science researcher is a philosopher, or someone who has rubbed shoulders with the philosopher*" (p. 237). This quote from van Manen invites us to observe that (human) research can be ascribed to a reflective/philosophical/methodical practice and tradition, in which "*a human science researcher*" takes part in and has the possibility to reflect over epistemological assumptions and the implications these have for empirical interpretations and analytical theorising. It is possible to regard this kind of epistemological immersion and reflection as an expression or as offspring of a Cartesian (methodological) attitude. Descartes (1985), on the subject of "method", says:

> *I mean reliable rules which are easy to apply, and such that if one follows them exactly, one will never take what is false to be true or fruitlessly expend one's mental efforts, but will gradually and constantly increase one's knowledge until one arrives at a true understanding of everything within one's capacity.*
>
> (p. 16)

Method understood in Cartesian terms such as these crystallise the importance of a correct application of reliable rules that eventually will result in "*a true understanding of everything within one's capacity*". In other words, a rigid and sticky sense of duty to the rules of the method will see to it or reassure the researcher that he is always on the right track. The intention behind this kind of Cartesian methodical reflection is undoubtedly motivated by, among other things, a need for a verifiable, predictable and reliable understanding whereby it is important to avoid being "thrown off-track" by random whims and seemingly non-essential empirical peculiarities that, in an undesired manner, force themselves on a predetermined methodological/ theoretic strategy.

While accepting that the Cartesian method can be deemed a useful and reliability-based reflective practice/discipline or tool by which to justify the function and legitimacy of the research being done, this kind of "reflection" does not necessarily exclude the possibility of revealing the radical, innate *indeterminacy* of research. The quote from van Manen (1989) may thus suggest something that can be claimed to be as important as the researcher's attention to predetermined methodological strategies, techniques and logical procedures.

In contrast, methodological approaches can be found that explicitly try to avoid *always too late*, for example by taking an auto-ethnographic, ethno-methodological position (Reinertsen, 2007), whereby the researcher defines himself as being in a position that always already is, and increasingly becomes, part of what is projected in the course of the research. In this respect, it is a question of process ontology whereby everything is recreated again and again. A journey is always already under way, a trip in differences – a non-preplanned itinerary.

Conversely, it may be that prior to data analysis and data collection, you as the researcher have thought through and ascertained that all the correct methodological and theoretical choices and rationales have been carried out, but that you do not understand that the field of research/practice that you are undertaking does not quite jibe with the original (theoretical) map that you designed. This may involve cherry-picking (i.e. selecting data that confirms existing theory and a predetermined analytical framework) and a dominant (unreflected) theory-directed research regime. Here too, it is possible to claim that in a sense, one is always too early. In other words, as a researcher, you are either always too late or always too early in the light of the unpleasant phantom of nothingness.

More concretely, we may be too late or too early when the following questions are posed: Are relevant quality criteria applied? Are there good correlations between theory and empiri? Has the right theory been chosen and how can we know this? Are these relevant empiri and sufficiently relevant empiri and how can we ensure this? Are the categories and systematisation of the empiri durable? Is the research too empiri-driven or too theory-directed? Should the research questions be changed? Have we chosen relevant subjects and informants? Are the data interpretations reasonable? What significant empiri are omitted as the research progresses, and what empiri are followed up and described in more detail? Can theory in empirical analyses and the theoretical framework for method use (methodology) be the same or different? From the outset, must a general theoretical perspective be selected in the form of a social-constructivist, positivist, or critical-realist point of view?

There may be grounds to track down and search for an awareness that can help to demonstrate the importance of the existential (nothing) dimension of the research. This entails an understanding that comes from the inside, that is, what is to be understood has to take its point of departure in one's own lived experiences with the discipline and scientific praxis. Research can be understood only as a stringently methodical science and as a systematically disciplined craft, but understanding of the "art", the personal engagement and the wonderment/stimulating aspects are also important. This entails that the research "requires" that one allows oneself to be challenged and that one is sensitive to the not-yet known and the labyrinths of the abyss, what Gadamer (1960) calls "the thing in itself". In this way, one can continually penetrate more deeply into the phenomenon and challenge one's own (self) understanding.

This may lead to the question of what form of "consciousness" we should make room for in higher education (and in research), if we wish to promote the "existential-nothing" dimension in qualitative research. Gadamer (1960) points out a whim-based and wonderment-based access that enables us to hear the voice not only of the discipline, the system and the other person but also of the "thing-in-itself".

This requires that we acknowledge that something "happens" in the creative and interpersonal relations and processes that routinely seem to elude our technical, systematic, conceptualising and methodological approaches. Nothing "consciousness" is to have an ear for this "extra" element and to allow this intangible nothing to make itself heard in an indirect manner.

Successful researchers do not wait until "the Muse kisses them" and gives them a "bright idea"; they go to work, they try to create new and different values and new and different satisfactions, to convert a "material" (data) into a "resource" (text), or to combine existing resources in a new configuration (Voice of Doing and Knowing). This is true, but it only half tells the story.

Perhaps this quote from Wittgenstein (1953) can illustrate the notion of "half the story":

> *Something that we know when no one asks us, but no longer know when we are supposed to give an account of it, is something that we need to remind ourselves of.*

(p. 43)

What we researchers can "remind ourselves of" to a greater extent are precisely the nothing experiences (cf. Chapter 7) that often lie baked into successful, challenging and stranded research alike. With the aid of a praxis of nothingness, it is possible to describe an approach that is linked not only with "the Voice of Knowing" and "the Voice of Doing" but also with "the Voice of Being-Nothing".

Implications of nothing for educational practice

"Show me Nothing", we might be tempted to say in an imperative tone.

Where is nothing? Disclose and find it! Show it to me, please! Otherwise, everything sounds like philosophical bullshit or at best nonsense and mumbo jumbo. If we assume its inherent hidden qualities, so what! what does it mean in practice? You might say, I want to know how to cease it? How to study it? Give me something concrete and point at that something and say, "Obviously this is nothing because . . ."! In other words, kindly operationalise "nothing" for me so that I will be able to implement it as a teacher and so that my students can handle it in terms of utility and effectiveness! Or even better, as a principal, I want to exhaustively implement the benefits of Nothing pedagogy as a new and better remedy for educational leadership, how?

First of all, I am not trying to mystify "nothing", but it is different from the traditional methodology of "operationalisation". Perhaps this quote might illuminate the issue:

> *The aspects of things that are most important for us are hidden because of their simplicity and familiarity. (One is unable to notice something – because it is always before one's eyes). The real foundations of his inquiry do not strike a man at all. Unless that fact has at some time struck him. – And this means; we fail to be struck by what, once seen, is most striking and most powerful.*

(Wittgenstein, 1953, paragraph 129)

Ludwig Wittgenstein is attempting in this quotation to direct the spotlight on what is perhaps the most important for us here in life, namely that which has a tendency to be concealed because of our everydayness, immediacy and simplicity. Therefore, we need to scrutinise praxis and what is always right before our eyes, and thereby perceive familiar and obvious terms as more complex and seductive than they frequently pass themselves off to be.

To some degree, Nothing surrounding us in our everyday being and life, in our being-in-the-world is often too common and too familiar to be noticed. Nothing is not manifested in the text or context but always already on the way to language and potential new self-understanding.

Let me provide a mundane example to indicate and hopefully engage you with what I mean:

Once at dinner the principal and two teachers at "Utility" high school met at a round table, the principal asked the two trusted and experienced teachers, Mary and Tom, why colleague Mummi, who is a novice teacher, suddenly stopped coming to work. This is a reconstruction of the conversation.

PRINCIPAL: I wonder why Mummi has stopped showing up at our place.

MARY: We (nodding at Tom) are not surprised. You called her inexperienced, little effective and a teacher with poor judgement the last time you spoke with her. She was upset. We think she probably still feels offended by you.

PRINCIPAL: Why would she become offended with me? She came to me with the latest evaluation report and asked my opinion. I told her my honest opinion, namely that her results are very poor. You know that I like to tell the goddamned truth to people's face. It's not my fault that she performed so poorly on that student evaluation.

TOM: You hurt her feelings. You didn't need to lie to Mummi, but you could at least have conveyed your truth to Mummi in a more considerate way. For example, you could have said something like, "It seems to me that you have some challenges with your teaching, no?"

PRINCIPAL: That would have been a lie. It did not "seem" to me; I saw it with my own eyes that she is too inexperienced. Not "a bit too inexperienced" but "very inexperienced"! Somebody has to tell her that.

MARY: From you as a principal, she wanted to hear a word of encouragement, not your offensive "truth".

PRINCIPAL: Truth can't be offensive. "Don't blame the mirror if your face is ugly!" If Mummi had wanted to hear a compliment, she should have gone to "friendly" behaving colleagues – not to me.

TOM: But admit it, you as principal don't like to hear the truth about yourself when it's unpleasant.

PRINCIPAL: I always love the truth, whatever it is. I always like when people tell me the truth, even when it is bitter.

MARY: Do you? What about when people say that you are instrumental, rude and insensitive?

PRINCIPAL: I don't like it because it is simply not true.

So, is it an example of a nothing and some kind of not-being-at-home experience? No, not by itself, until it starts to be puzzling and awakening to you as a reader. It interests me. I wonder if the principal's logic is based on some kind of logical fallacy that grants her the right to tell unpleasant "techno-truth" to others while rejecting this right when "techno-truth" is presented by others to herself (imagine a job satisfaction report where the behaviour of the principal is labelled as a rude and insensitive style of leadership). It seems the logic is OK – it is consistent and correct, but logic, itself, is not omnipotent in educational practice.

I wonder if the principal would agree that truth can't be rude and insensitive, that rudeness is based on meanness while insensitivity is based on wrong perception. In light of maxims of proper communication, the principal was not mean-spirited but rather sincere and useful to Mummi (remember Grice's maxims of good communication: be truthful, be informative, be relevant and be clear, Grice, 1975). Arguably, the principal properly observed all these maxims in communication with Mummi, but it can be argued that it was not enough. Or that something else is at stake. Of course, besides truth, one can be concerned about the psychological well-being of another person, or about being potentially more appreciative of another's labour, as in the case of Mummi. Of course, the concern about truth can overweigh these non-truth concerns. At least, this "something else" has to be considered when a person provides a response. However, it is interesting in this example that Mary and Tom chose the principal's own way of delivering "techno-truth" to communicate with her about the drawbacks in this way of relating with students (as may be indicated by job satisfaction and evaluation reports). Mary and Tom were telling the principal *their* bitter "techno-truth" directly to her face when offering possible reasons for why Mummi stopped showing up. Not only did the principal use her logical closed-circuit to respond to Mary and Tom, but they also used logical closed-circuit to address her and show the limitations of using closed-circuit and report-launched endpoints. The difference was that the principal believed in using logical/clear-cut closed-circuit technology, but the teachers did not. Were the teachers hypocritical?

Can nothing "issues" be scrutinised and talked through using logic? Could Mary and Tom have presented their objections to the principal in a different way without using her telling techno-truth-to-your-face logical way? If so, what way might it be? Should teachers tell their students technological-truth about their deficits (lack of preparation regarding curriculum, lack of engagement in supervision and learning situations, poor grades, etc.) to their face? Why? Why not? What are alternatives? Finally (for now), does presentation of truth affect the truth itself and potentially invoke the uncanny nothing-in-techno-truths? I use this example because I thought it would be easier to be engaged by nothing in an awaiting (but I could be wrong – if so, sorry).

However, philosophies of Wittgenstein and Heidegger use very mundane and trivial examples to indicate and open up the potential of "hidden" everydayness and Nothing. Moreover, this experience is always possible for Dasein (human understanding) and it does not need an unusual event to arouse it, because, "*its sway is as thorough going as its possible occasionings are trivial. It is always ready, though it only seldom springs, and we are snatched away and left hanging*" (Heidegger, 1993, p. 93).

With these words in mind, it seems very hard to "pedagogise" nothing educational practice without throwing out the baby with the bathwater. But let's try.

The defining characteristic of a technological lesson is the teacher's act of presetting an endpoint. Still, whether the endpoint is preset at the start of the lesson or not is not the discriminating characteristic between a technological lesson and a nothing lesson. A Nothing lesson needs some preset endpoint (most often set by teachers). What makes this lesson nothing-like, but not technological, is that the first preset endpoint is not an answer but a question. For a lesson to invite to nothing experiences, there should be a genuine question at the beginning. That question ignites the inquiry process in the class and makes the lesson nothing-"prepared". The question should not be the so-called known-information-question that the teacher knows the answer, but should be instead the one I call the unknown-information-seeking-question where the teacher does not know the answer before the class.

Another characteristic of a nothing-inviting lesson is that the question changes throughout the lesson. In other words, both students and teachers, through their common nothing experience, discover new questions or new implications deriving from the first question throughout the lesson. Nothing questioning unfinalises itself and the inquiry. This is perhaps the real hallmark of a nothing pedagogical lesson.

In summary, to strive for nothing pedagogical lessons in higher education seems to demand a shift from strategically prioritising the definition of a human being as "knowing-the-world" (i.e. epistemological priority) or "serving-some-other-outcomes" (the instrumental priority) rather than "being-in-the-world".

References

Aristotle. (1988). *Nichomachean Ethic*. New York: Dover Publications.

Descartes, R. (1985). *The Philosophical Writings of Descartes*. Cambridge: Cambridge University Press.

Gadamer, H. G. (1960). *Truth and Method*. London: Continuum International Publishing Group Ltd.

Grice, H. P. (1975). Logic and Conservation. In *Speech Acts* (pp. 41–58). Boston: Brill.

Heidegger, M. (1962). *Being and Time*. New York: Harper & Row.

Heidegger, M. (1993). Was is Metaphysik?. In M. Heidegger (Ed.), *Wegmarken, Gesamtausgabe* (V. Klostermann, Trans.). Frankfurt: Vittorio Klostermann.

Piaget, J. (1953). *The Origin of Intelligence in the Child*. London: Routledge & Kegan & Paul.

Polanyi, M. (2002). *Personal Knowledge: Towards a Post-critical Epistemology*. London: Routledge.

Reinertsen, A. (2007). *Spunk–A Love Story. Teacher Community Not*. Doctoral thesis, Norwegian University of Science and Technology. Retrieved from https://ntnuopen.ntnu.no/ntnu-xmlui/handle/11250/269142.

Raynes, S. & Rutledge, A., (2010). *Elements of Structured Finance*. Oxford: Oxford University Press.

van Manen, M. (1989). *Researching Lived Experience: Human Science for an Action Sensitive Pedagogy*. London: Althouse Press.

Whitehead, A. (1938). *Modes of Thought*. New York: The Free Press.

Wittgenstein, L. (1953). *Philosophische Untersuchungen* (Translated as *Philosophical Investigations* [in German and English], Rev. 4th ed., by G. E. M. Anscombe, P. M. S. Hacker, & J. Schulte). Chichester, West Sussex, UK and Malden, MA: Wiley-Blackwell, 2009.

Index

For Product Safety Concerns and Information please contact our EU
representative GPSR@taylorandfrancis.com Taylor & Francis Verlag GmbH,
Kaufingerstraße 24, 80331 München, Germany

Printed and bound by CPI Group (UK) Ltd, Croydon, CR0 4YY

11/04/2025

01844011-0004